GW00750744

797,885 Books

are available to read at

www.ForgottenBooks.com

Forgotten Books' App
Available for mobile, tablet & eReader

ISBN 978-1-332-21949-0
PIBN 10300023

English
Français
Deutsche
Italiano
Español
Português

www.forgottenbooks.com

Mythology Photography **Fiction**
Fishing Christianity **Art** Cooking
Essays Buddhism Freemasonry
Medicine **Biology** Music **Ancient**
Egypt Evolution Carpentry Physics
Dance Geology **Mathematics** Fitness
Shakespeare **Folklore** Yoga Marketing
Confidence Immortality Biographies
Poetry **Psychology** Witchcraft
Electronics Chemistry History **Law**
Accounting **Philosophy** Anthropology
Alchemy Drama Quantum Mechanics
Atheism Sexual Health **Ancient History**
Entrepreneurship Languages Sport
Paleontology Needlework Islam
Metaphysics Investment Archaeology
Parenting Statistics Criminology
Motivational

A COMPLETE WORK

ON

THE PRUNING OF
FRUIT TREES.

By JAS. F. MOODY,

FRUIT INDUSTRIES COMMISSIONER,
WESTERN AUSTRALIA.

Price 3s. 6d.

PERTH:
BY AUTHORITY: FRED. WM. SIMPSON, GOVERNMENT PRINTER.
1912.

JAS. F. MOODY

FRUIT INDUSTRIES COMMISSIONER.

Late Manager Toomuc Valley Orchards, Pakenham, Vic.

Orchardist and Irrigationist.
Kameruka Estate
Bega, N.S.W.

INDEX.

INTRODUCTORY.

To

THE HON. THE MINISTER FOR AGRICULTURE.

In offering this work on pruning to the growers of Western Australia I am giving them the benefit of my own practical experience extending over 20 years, and the principles laid down have been gained by close observation of the different varieties. That the system adopted has proved most successful in making trees bear heavy crops of fruit can be substantiated by those who have known me both in New South Wales and Victoria. During the past ten years I have not only carefully watched the results and improved on them, but have taken photos. showing the trees at different stages, and my plates now number some hundreds.

Having gained my experience in different districts and parts of both New South Wales and Victoria it has taught me how necessary it is for the orchardist to always study local conditions, and in many ways I have had to change my system or modify it on moving into a new district where the climatic and soil conditions were totally different.

In this work, I have as far as possible taken into consideration any such local conditions as my short residence in the Western State has permitted me to become acquainted with, and later on, when I know more about these local conditions, I may have to revise this work, but the general principles laid-down hold good all the world over, and the practical grower can use them while adopting any particular method he has proved suitable to his locality.

I have freely illustrated this work, because being a practical man myself I know how quickly others can grasp ideas when put before them in an illustrated way, also beginners can more quickly follow the reading matter.

I wish growers to fully recognise that to get the highest financial results from the methods of pruning I advocate, they must carefully avoid repeating the same mistakes that have been made in the Eastern States, for most failures in fruit growing can be laid to mistakes, neglect, carelessness, or ignorance on the growers' part. They must also be prepared to practise intense culture, for trees cannot carry the heavy crops of the quality here illustrated, unless well manured and irrigated, when necessary. In practically all the most suitable parts of Western Australia for fruit growing, provision can be made for irrigating by storage dams as is done in several of the Victorian fruit districts. I would urge the following on the grower :—

" i." Select the site and soil of the future plantation carefully.

" ii." Clear the land well, getting out all roots and stumps (a source very often of serious trouble later), plough deeply or subsoil.

6

" iii." Drain wherever necessary.

" iv." Lay out the orchard well, so as to cultivate at all angles and save manual labour.

" v." Choose your trees carefully, stock and variety suited to the district only being selected, and see that the trees are well grown and free from all diseases, and select the best commercial export varieties only for your " main " plantation.

" vi." Keep the tree strong and vigorous from the start, feeding it well.

" vii." Cultivate deeply and frequently.

" viii." Manure heavily when the trees bear heavily ; it is money well spent.

" ix." Never allow a tree to overbear, but let it carry all it can without distress and without losing quality or size.

" x." Make provision for irrigating whenever possible.

" xi." Don't plant a bigger area than you have capital to manage thoroughly.

" xii." Keep your framework and leaders right through the tree's existence. If these twelve rules are well observed, I do not think the grower will have cause to complain about the financial results from any plantation. My object all through has been to place the matter as clearly and simply as possible before the reader, and I trust my efforts will be appreciated.

JAS. F. MOODY,
Fruit Industries Commissioner.

Department of Agriculture,
Perth, Western Australia, 1912.

THE PRUNING of FRUIT TREES.

Pruning Tools.

Beginners often require information as to the tools necessary for pruning.

Figure I. shows two forms of pruning saws, these have a bow of steel and a thin steel blade with keen teeth. They are most suitable for cutting large or

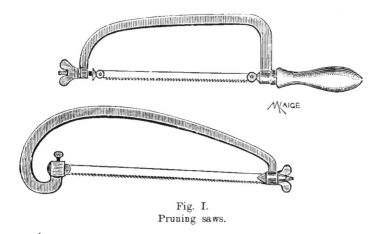

Fig. I.
Pruning saws.

small limbs. They can be adjusted to any angle and make a very clean, rapid cut. The blade can be inserted to cut either by drawing to the operator or by pushing

Fig. II.
Pruning knife.

from him, the former method being the best ; spare blades can be obtained. The saw cuts must be trimmed smooth, otherwise the wound does not heal over. Figure III. illustrates a Depôse secateurs, while Figure IV. illustrates two other makes of secateurs and a large two-handed secateurs, used principally in vine pruning,

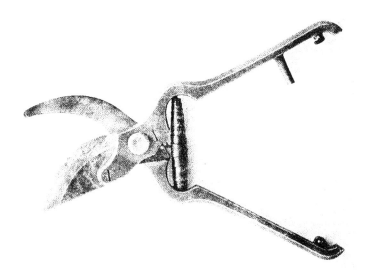

Fig. III.
A pair of Depôse secateurs.

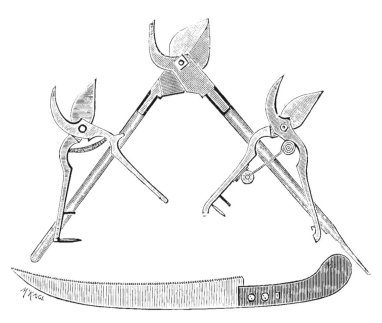

Fig. IV.
Pruning tools.

when heavy stubs or old arms have to be removed. The pruning saw shown at the foot of Figure IV. is a Wingfield, which is much used, and by some operators preferred to the frame saws. Figure V. illustrates a long pruning shear mounted on a light pole about eight feet long. It is chiefly used in pruning hedges and or-

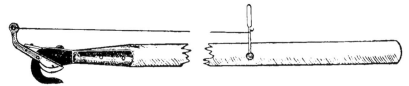

Fig. V.
Pruning shear for hedges, etc.

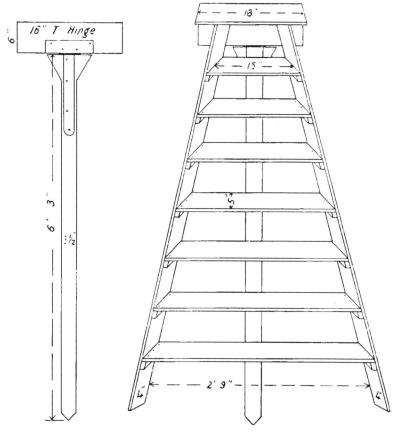

Fig. VI.
Orchard ladder.

námental trees. All tools must be kept very sharp, well oiled and clean. Figure VI. shows a very suitable orchard ladder with only one leg behind, which can be pushed down between limbs or into the centre of the tree without doing any damage. There are many brands of secateurs on the market, the Wiss, the Mexeur, and the Rieser being among the best, while the Depôse is a cheap and very satisfactory tool. These secateurs can be obtained in various sizes and spare parts are to be obtained for them. The steel wire coil and the steel telescope are the best forms of springs, and spare ones should always be on hand. When using the secateurs the blunt lower jaw should never be allowed to come in contact with the bud, this blunt portion of the secateurs always leaves a slight bruise on the stem, and for this reason—whether the secateurs are held with the blade up or downwards the blade should always be next to the portion of the limb or part remaining on the tree, the blunt portion of the secateurs coming in contact with the portion of the tree removed. If this practice is always observed the bruise will be on the portion of the tree removed, leaving a clean cut behind. A strong, wide-mouthed pair of secateurs, with a good hook, will cut a limb over an inch in diameter if the operator pushes the limb to be cut away from the blade when using the secateurs. If this is done properly there is no necessity to work the secateurs up and down as is often done, damaging the bark so badly that the wound does not heal over readily.

🔲 🔲 🔲 🔲

The Parts of the Tree.

Many growers find the terms used in describing pruning very confusing, so I have included a few remarks on this subject.

The Tap Root is the main centre root of the tree; this root should always be cut back when planting so as to promote lateral root growth and good bearing habits in the tree.

The lateral roots are those thrown out laterally by the tree.

The secondary roots are the branches from the lateral roots.

The fibrous roots are the fine rootlets thrown off from the lateral and secondary roots.

The root hairs are the minute hairs thrown off by the fibrous roots; these supply the nutriment to the tree in a soluble form. These fine hair rootlets penetrate in all directions between the soil particles and absorb the moisture through the cap cells at their extremities and transfer it to the tree above, where it is elaborated by the foliage in conjunction with the carbonic acid absorbed by the stomata or mouths of the leaves into the material used in building up the parts of the tree and fruit. the chlorophyll or green colouring matter in the foliage aiding in this assimilation process which can only take place in sunlight, therefore during the day time.   .

It is considered that the crude sap rises by osmotic or cell pressure chiefly through the sapwood, the water being evaporated through the foliage; the nutriment required for the building up the parts of the tree, after being manufactured in the foliage. is distributed during the night to the different parts of the tree. Those substances not required or of a poisonous nature are either exuded on the outer covering of the tree or returned to the roots with the downward flow of sap, chiefly through the inner bark and exuded by the roots as humic or toxic substances.

The trunk is the main stem of the tree.

The main arms are the first main branches from the trunk or stem formed in the first pruning.

The secondary arms are the branches or subdivisions thrown off the main arms.

The leaders are the main branches off the subarms; in other words the -eading shoots. which become the permanent leaders.   ·

The laterals are lateral ·growths from the main arms, sub-arms, and leaders.

Lateral spurs are spurs developed on the lateral growth.

Spurs are short growths from the arms, loaders, or laterals, containing fruit buds.

Ramified spurs.—A fruit spur which has increased and multiplied as the tree aged.

Terminals refer to the extremities of the leaders or laterals.

Terminal bud.—The bud at the extremity of a leader or lateral.

Terminal shoot.—The shoot at the extremity of a leader or lateral.

Buds.—The dormant flower. leaf or wood bud usually found at regular intervals along the wood growth and at the extremities. These are found at the base of the leaf. The buds are classed as :—*wood-buds*, those which will throw a shoot in the Spring ; a *leaf bud*, one which only produces leaves ; and a *flower bud* one which produces a flower or fruit.

Node.—The node is a slight swelling where a leaf is produced during the growth of the shoot ; at each leaf a bud is produced. and in some plants. such as a vine, a division occurs in the growth.

Internode is the space between two buds.

The leaf forms the foliage of the plant or tree.

Outer bark is the outer covering of the tree which has been hardened by the exuding of calcium salts. This hard covering forms the protection to the tree.

New bark is the ring of new bark found just under the outer bark through which the downward flow of sap mostly takes place.

Cambium layer is the inner covering next to the sapwood.

Sapwood is the younger wood covered by the cambium layer through which the upward flow of sap chiefly travels.

Woody fibre is the old woody formation of the tree.

Pith is the soft material usually found in a tube in the centre of the heartwood.

🌀 🌀 🌀 🌀

Time for Pruning.

The winter pruning should be done during June, July. and August, and the early part of September, and should finish before the buds burst—July and August being the best months for this work.

The early varieties of peaches, and those varieties which shed their buds, and also those apricots which show the same fault, should not be winter-pruned until the pink of the flower-bud shows, otherwise all the fruit may be cut off.

No hard-and-fast rule can be laid down, for each variety acts differently, according to the season. For instance, even the Goldmine Nectarine this season (1912) in some districts threw its buds, and yet this variety as a rule is a sure cropper.

I would advise not pruning peaches until late in the season—about the end of August. The pruner, by giving the tree or the limb a vigorous shake, will then be able to tell whether the buds are sound ; if faulty, they will fall in a shower.

Many varieties of young trees require both summer and winter pruning of top as well as laterals ; apricots, and some of the plums belong to this class. Other varieties of fruits require summer pruning or nipping of the laterals, the top growth being thinned out and the permanent leaders left intact. Summer pruning of young trees should be done early in the season, about November–December, as this permits the new top growth to mature thoroughly before the fall. It is further necessary to summer-prune the lateral growth again, about March.

Early peaches and apricots which throw their buds should have the lateral growth summer-pruned after the fruit has been harvested. ·

Young pears should have the lateral growth treated twice during the summer —early and late.

All varieties of bearing trees which require summer treatment of their lateral growth should be summer-pruned about the end of February or early in March.

🔯 🔯 🔯 🔯

Remarks on Pruning to inside Buds in order to spread the Tree.

Some pruners are practising pruning to inside buds in order to spread trees. The top bud always takes the sap and makes the strongest shoot, and, if pruned close, will grow straight up. On the other hand, the second bud, which is on the outside, makes a weaker shoot at a wide angle, because the wood above prevents it from growing upright. Removing the first or inside shoot, and throwing the

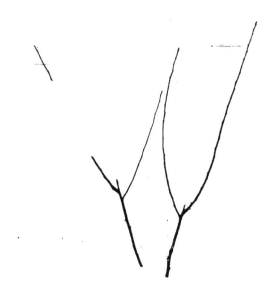

Pruning to inside buds.

leader into the wide but weak second shoot, will certainly cause the tree to spread ; but I am entirely opposed to the principle, for there is too much risk attached to its practice, as it is noticeable that in the case of young trees the second bud does not always shoot. Should the second bud fail to shoot, the grower is in a most unfortunate position ; he has ruined his tree for good by throwing the shoot inward. During this season, in two districts, I came across trees which, as the result of this practice, had been thrown inwards instead of outwards.

Where an outside lateral happens on upright growers, by all means make use of it to form a fork or to widen the base by throwing the leaders into the lateral ; but I caution growers not to make a practice of pruning to inside buds with the object of widening the base of the tree. Get all the strength and growth possible into your main leaders, and this you can do with certainty only by obtaining the growth on the terminal bud left in the previous pruning of the leader. There is, besides, no necessity for the practice of pruning to an inside bud in order to spread the tree, for you can obtain the required results from the top outside bud if the shoot is pruned well above, although it will not throw so wide as the weaker lower shoot. When the leader is pruned close to the bud, the shoot goes straight up, perpendicular to its parent ; but if the leader is pruned well above the required bud, pruning just below the bud above it, the shoot cannot grow straight up, and is forced out at a wider angle, just as a lateral shoot grows ; the angle at which the top shoot grows being governed entirely by the strength of the shoot. The illustration shows limbs pruned well above the bud : the second bud has certainly thrown wider owing to its being of weaker growth.

I trust, therefore, growers will consider this sure and safe method of directing growth in place of the risky one. I have always succeeded in spreading my base by pruning well above the bud. Let any grower pause and study the illustration, and he will at once recognise that it is impossible for the bud to grow at any but a wide angle with the strip of wood above the bud. In these illustrations the top shoots are particularly vigorous, being four feet long, and half-inch in diameter at the base of the new wood. The stub shown must, of course, be removed in the following winter.

NOTE.—If it is necessary to throw a leading shoot wide, whether outwards for an upright grower, or inwards for a wide grower, prune well above the bud, so as to leave a bare stub at least one inch long. If requiring to grow the leading shoot straight up, perpendicular to its parent stem, prune close to the bud. The reason why a lateral grows at a wide angle to its parent stem is simply that the wood above prevents its growth in an upright direction. A stub of a quarter of an inch in length above the bud will throw the shoot only slightly out, but a stub one inch long will throw the shoot well out, the angle of its growth being governed by the strength of the shoot.

🌿 🌿 🌿 🌿

Objects of Pruning.

The objects of pruning are to regulate fruit-production both as to quality and quantity, and to extend the tree's productiveness over long periods.

Nature, if left to herself, seeks merely to reproduce herself, and the tree, unless assisted by intelligent help, generally lacks quality in its production and gradually goes back in regularity of bearing, eventually producing unpalatable and inferior fruit ; and the tree soon becomes a wreck.

Intelligent pruning and cultivation are practised with the object of improving on Nature and keeping her up' to a high standard of perfection.

No tree can be pruned by rule-of-thumb. Locality, soil, and climatic conditions must be studied. A good pruner will study the 'requirements of the tree to be treated, together with local conditions. He must understand circulation of sap, balance of root and top, action of light ar.. air, and the necessity for keeping a good, stout framework in order to meet the requirements of economically working and harvesting the crop, as well as spacing of the leaders to carry the laterals and give the tree free circulation of air and sunlight for the healthy maturing of both wood and fruit.

The closest attention must be given to having the tree sufficiently open in the centre, and yet not too open ; the centre should be hollow, and no more. Many growers in this State have their trees far too open and without sufficient leaders. The tree, if a wide grower, can carry from 18 to 24 main leaders comfortably, whilst an upright grower can carry 15 or 18 main leaders. These leaders should form a double row right round the circumference of the tree, and should be placed with ample intervening spaces, so that sun and light will have free entry ; yet it must be borne in mind that too much sun must not be permitted to play on the bark or the fruit, as this would cause the fruit to scald and the tree to become bark-bound. The latter trouble is indicated by a hard or red appearance of the bark, and its effects are to interfere with the sap-flow, so that the spurs are not properly nourished and the wood-growth becomes poor and weak. In pruning, one should always consider how the tree will appear when in foliage, and one should give sufficient space only, according to variety, to clothe the tree amply with foliage, without sheltering the fruit too much (as this would prevent its colouring up well), yet at the same time not failing to protect both bark and fruit thoroughly from sun-scald.

The foliage also has another and important function : the assimilation process. This is a very important duty, on the proper performance of which the entire growth and productiveness of the tree depend. The foliage absorbs from the air the carbonic acid needed for building up the parts of the tree and the fruit. This carbonic acid is converted by the leaves, in conjunction with the nutriment supplied by the roots, into starch, sugar, cellulose, fats, tissues, acid, all woody fibres, bark, spurs, buds, etc., necessary for the building-up of the tree and fruit ; the foliage acting as a veritable laboratory during the process.

From the foregoing it will be recognised how very necessary it is to provide ample foliage and to keep that foliage healthy during the spring and summer months.

When summer pruning is practised, care and judgment must be used not to remove too much foliage, otherwise serious harm will result to the tree and crop.

It is very essential that the tree be kept thoroughly vigorous at all times. No matter what quantity of fruit it may be carrying, at least one foot to 18 inches of top growth on each of the leaders must be maintained to keep the tree healthy. This top growth not only ensures the sap being drawn to the extremities of the limbs, but maintains a healthy sap-flow throughout the tree ; and this, again, ensures not only the thorough nourishment of all fruit, but the complete develop-ment and maturing of spur and bud formation for the following season's fruit. Unless proper attention is given to maintaining the healthy sap-flow, the best results cannot be obtained. With scalded bark and no top-growth, a healthy flow of sap is not possible.

The trees must be kept in a healthy growing state right through the summer. The practice of discontinuing the cultivation as soon as the fruit has matured is not a wise one, especially in a climate where no summer rains fall, for the tree becomes semi-dormant if the nourishment fails ; and when the rains do come late in autumn, the tree is apt to start a second growth or come in flower out of season. Besides it is impossible to mature the spurs if moisture fails too early.

It must be borne in mind that the tree has not only to mature its fruit, but to develop its spur growth and fruit-buds as well. Apart from this fact, the last action of a tree before going dormant in the late autumn is to store up in its tissues (*i.e.*, the cambium layer, or inner bark), and in the spurs and buds and roots, sufficient nutriment to start the tree off in the spring. To note this action of a tree is most important ; for not only does the following fruit-crop depend on the fruit-buds being developed up nice and plump, but the spring growth depends on the store of nutriment held in the tissues of the trees. A good orchardist can generally tell from the development of the buds what sort of a crop he is likely to have, and he manures accordingly. If he expects a heavy crop, he will fertilise heavily to meet the tree's coming demands, never permitting the tree to become so exhausted as to be unable to mature spur and bud formation for the following season's crop. It is essential, therefore, that deep and constant cultivation be maintained through the summer months, to supply the necessary moisture. If the moisture fails, no amount of fertiliser is of any value, for the tree cannot take up nourishment except in a soil-water soluble form, and cannot make use of it unless the foliage is sufficient and healthy.

Pruning.

When planting a young fruit-tree, of no matter what variety,[1] always remove the centre leader. Choose well-grown yearling trees, from a reliable nurseryman, and see that they are free from all disease. The main stem should be short—not more than 18 inches high. Select three well-placed arms starting from different portions of the main stem, at a wide angle if possible, and remove all others. Shorten the three arms back to three or four buds, pruning to an outside bud or to a bud which will throw the shoot in the required direction, the object being to form a wide, stout base of main arms to build the future tree upon ; these main arms jointing at different parts round the trunk give a very strong base.

Fig. 1.
Planting the tree.

Figure 1 shows how the tree should be planted ; Figure 2 shows the correct depth to plant, and Figure 3 shows the correct way to prune the young tree.

Upon these the sub-arms and leaders are built in the form of an inverted cone, with no centre leader. The tree must be kept well balanced on all sides. The centre hollow, with a double row of leaders evenly placed all round, must show no crowding anywhere. Figure 4 represents (" a " and " b ") two young apples unpruned, and (" c " and " d ") two young peaches unpruned. Figure 5 shows these same trees pruned.

Fig. 2.
Correct depth to plant.

Fig. 3.
Correct way to prune the young tree.

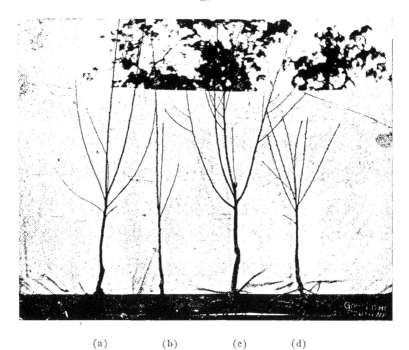

(a) (b) (c) (d)

Fig. 4.

Showing (a) and (b), two young Apples, and (c) and
(d), two young Peaches.

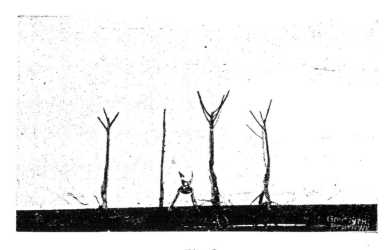

Fig. 5.

The same trees pruned.

All roots should be trimmed, but not cut short ; only the extremities should be cut where jagged by the spade in digging up. Cut out any bruised, broken, or damaged roots, and shorten in any long ones before planting. Figure 6 shows how a " whip " should be pruned when planting. Should a tree have all its shoots bunched up together, then every shoot except the centre one should be removed and the young tree cut as in Figure 5, " b." These trees can then be formed in the following winter. The following winter, which is considered the first pruning (the tree now being one year old from planting), the tree is again pruned hard, about 6in. to 9in. being left, and the arms being thrown as wide as possible. In wide-growing varieties obtain forks where possible, but do not fork upright growers until the second year's pruning, otherwise the base of the tree is too cramped. Narrow-growing trees can often be spread by cutting out the leaders to an outside lateral and throwing the growth into the lateral. Figure 7 illustrates the first year's pruning of a well-forked tree.

Fig. 6.
Pruning a whip.

Fig. 7.
First year's pruning of a young tree.

In the second year's pruning the trees are again pruned hard, about nine inches to one foot being left, and a well-placed fork being obtained on each of last year's pruning, which will give from six to eight or more leaders, according to variety and growth of the tree. Remove all but a few laterals from the inside of the tree ; also thin out any excess of laterals on the outside of the limbs and slightly shorten back those left.

In the third winter's pruning, prune fairly hard, leaving up to 18 inches on each leader, and obtaining a well-placed fork on each, which will now give from 12 to 16 leaders.

Practically all trees are treated in this manner for the first three years so as to obtain a strong open framework. Some varieties, such as the apricot and various plums and prunes, are improved by summer pruning ; but each of these will be treated under its own heading.

In the fourth pruning, forks are again left if sufficient leaders have not already been obtained. As a rule 15 to 18 are left on the pear and on all upright growers, and from 18 to 24 on wide-growing varieties are ample, and then no crowding results. Any crowding of the top of the tree means starvation and barrenness of the base and main arms, because sunlight and air must be given free circulation throughout the tree in order to keep the lower fruiting-wood strong, healthy, and productive.

We now have the framework of our tree, and each variety of fruit must be treated and studied separately and pruned to suit its particular requirements. When once the requisite number of leaders has been obtained, no further forks or branches are permitted, unless to fill up a space caused by a broken limb and so forth, and the leaders must be kept intact so as to draw the sap direct to the extremities. Once the leaders are lost, the grower is soon in difficulties ; for he has lost, with them, control of the tree, and the extremities are converted into fruiting wood.

After the third year we have to consider our future crops of fruit and throw the tree into bearing. This must be done gradually, as the young tree must not be exhausted by being made to bear heavy crops but should be gradually brought into full bearing as it approaches and reaches the age of eight or ten years, according to variety ; the object being to maintain a strong, healthy, and vigorous low-set tree, capable of bearing regular and heavy crops of fruit from base upwards, on the framework or leaders established, without any breaking-down of the limbs or stunting of the tree, this framework being so well spaced as to allow plenty of room between each leader, and the centre of the tree being kept as well open as the variety and climatic conditions require, and all the main and secondary arms being at an angle and not upright to the trunk.

The fruiting wood or spurs should be built up gradually each year on all varieties of trees.

The Apple.

Having obtained the frame work of the tree, the laterals having been thinned and shortened each year are now allowed to go unpruned on those varieties which carry their fruits on the lateral growth. This checks their growth, and has the additional advantage of throwing all the strength of the tree into the main leaders. These laterals, if left unpruned, in some varieties in one year, in others in two years, develop fruit-buds along their full length. These laterals must then be shortened back, and only permitted length enough to carry and mature only good quality fruit, as local conditions permit. In some strong-growing varieties it is necessary to allow the leaders also to go unshortened, but whenever this is done the leaders should be shortened back the following winter to strengthen them, otherwise they become too weak and willowy to carry future crops. This process should not be practised until the fourth or fifth year, according to the vigour and size of the tree, and only then if all the leaders required have already been obtained, and the process must be repeated until the tree is thrown into bearing habits by checking the wood growth and promoting fruiting spurs. By letting the leaders go in this manner every bud along the leader develops into a fruit-bud, but provided the tree is vigorous no hesitation need be made in shortening the leader back, for the terminal buds will burst and continue the leaders. This applies equally to the pear and plum as to the apple. *Jonathan leaders must never be allowed to go unshortened each winter pruning*, not only because it is unnecessary with this variety, but, more important still, because it so weakens the leaders that it is difficult to get strength into them again; they will bear fruit to the extremities and break down, or the tree becomes a dislocated wreck so far as shape and form is concerned.

Such varieties as the Rome Beauty do not spur on the laterals if they are left unpruned, but only on the tips, therefore, none but the short laterals should be left unshortened. They make strong lateral growth after each winter pruning, but can be thrown into bearing by judicious summer pruning of the laterals. *The leaders of apple trees should never be summer pruned, only the lateral growth.* Other varieties are naturally prolific and form their spurs readily unaided, and the laterals can be short pruned during the winter as they spur readily under this treatment, but in all " Natural Spurrers," such as Dunn's Seedling, Five Crown, Statesman, Cleopatra, Rokewood, and others of the same class, consideration must be given to the due protection of the bark of the tree from sunscald mentioned before and to allow sufficient foliage for the assimilation process. It is therefore very necessary to leave longer laterals at regular intervals up the leaders so as to provide the necessary foliage, for it must be remembered that these natural spurs are only short pointed spurs until the tree ages, and as each carries a fruit or two with perhaps only two or three leaves close into the leader, very little foliage is provided either for shelter or for the assimilation process. A good, vigorous, healthy tree will bear in its fourth or fifth year, and only a little fruit should be permitted before this age is reached, or otherwise serious harm will result by stunting its growth, and the grower will pay dearly who tries to make a tree productive before it reaches an age when it may be productive without distress. The crop can be gradually increased each year until the tree is carrying up to its full capacity.

After the fourth year the leaders are left longer (if not permitted to go unpruned for a season) in pruning so as to gradually decrease the wood growth and throw the vigour of the tree (which must be kept up) into fruit production, but the leaders must never be allowed to become too weak and willowy to carry their fruit, and no fruit must be permitted on the tops of the leaders until they are strong enough to carry the weight without breaking or becoming distorted. Once the tree has reached a suitable height and begins to bear good crops of fruit, the leaders should be hard pruned so as to maintain the top growth, because the maturing of the fruit will now check the excess of wood growth.

The Jonathan.—This tree requires more skill in pruning than most varieties, but no apple repays proper handling better. It is very often necessary to prune the Jonathan to inside buds or to an upright lateral to prevent the tree from spreading too wide. The laterals (and leaders) should only be shortened to good stout buds, as the first two are invariably blind. Figures 8 and 9 show a well grown three-year old Jonathan, unpruned and pruned. It will be seen, although the tree is only three years old, that a number of leaders have already been obtained, there being 12 in the illustration, and a few more will be added during the fourth pruning, bringing the number up to about 18 or 24 in all, the number being dependent on the spread of the tree. It will be noticed how well spaced these leaders are, no crowding, ample space being left not only in the centre of the tree, but also between each leader, with plenty of room for the lateral growth so necessary for this variety to bear its fruit upon ; the long laterals have been shortened in, especially those towards the tops of the leaders, while shorter ones of lighter wood have not been cut back. It is not advisable to form too many fruiting spurs on such a young tree, especially on the extremities of the leaders; these spurs are gradually built up each year, a greater number being left unpruned each winter. In this way the bearing capacity of the tree is not overtaxed but gradually built up from year to year ; each season the spurs on the previous year's wood being formed so that no fruit is allowed on the tops of the leaders until they are strong enough to support the fruit. This is most necessary in the Jonathan because

Fig. 8.
Three-year Jonathan unpruned.

Fig. 9.
Three-year-old Jonathan pruned.

the leaders do not obtain the necessary strength as quickly as other varieties. Those laterals left unpruned are shortened back when the fruit spurs are formed

24

each season, from four to eight buds being left, according to the number of spurs and their strength and the requirements of the tree. As soon as we have the required number of leaders they are not again forked or branched in pruning but kept intact right through, the extremities being kept clear of all lateral growth so as to ensure a clean get away of the shoot. This process is continued each year, the leaders kept strong and vigorous, and the laterals kept healthy, strong, and productive by shortening in after they form fruit-buds. The laterals must be shortened in the following year after being left unpruned, more especially the longer ones, not only because the tree will overbear, but each lateral will soon become barren

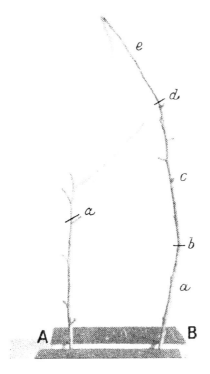

Fig. 10.
Jonathan laterals.

near its base in place of increasing and multiplying. Figure 10 shows, "A," a Jonathan lateral which was allowed to go unpruned the previous winter. It will be noticed that the wood-buds along its full length have been converted into fruit spurs. This lateral should be shortened back where marked (a) to strengthen the spurs, otherwise the wood will become barren after bearing. " B " illustrates how the laterals become barren if not shortened back. (a) shows three year-old wood quite barren owing to not having been shortened back ; this should have been cut where marked at (b) ; (c) shows two-year old growth with developed spurs, and this if not cut back where marked (d) will also become barren ; (e) shows last year's growth.   Figure 11 shows the four-year old tree pruned, while Figure 12 shows a five-year old tree unpruned, and Figure 12A the same tree pruned. Figures 13 and 14 show the nine-year old Jonathan unpruned and pruned built up in this manner.   It will be seen how prolific in fruiting wood the tree has become and how strong and healthy ; also how well balanced the tree is.   This tree has 24 main leaders and yet there is no crowding, not only have we an open centre, but ample room is provided between the leaders for the carrying of the laterals and the free entry of sunlight and air.   The tree is well clothed with fruiting wood from the base up without excess or crowding.   This tree was pruned from the

Fig. 11.
Four-year old Jonathan pruned.

ground without the aid of a ladder and bore the previous season six cases of first class export fruit.   Figure 15 shows the tree in foliage ; some fruit is permitted towards the top but the leaders are carrying the fruit without difficulty.   One of the chief aims of a good orchardist is to keep the spur growth round the bases of all trees healthy and productive, and this can only be done by properly nourishing the tree, by the free entry of air and sunlight, and by judicious pruning.   Figure 16 shows the base of a 23-year old Jonathan clothed with fruit and making good lateral growth.   Figure 17 shows a portion of a 15-year old Jonathan carrying 10 cases of fruit.

Fig. 12A.
The same tree pruned.

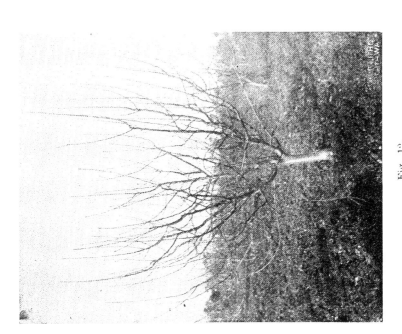

Fig. 12.
Unpruned five-year Jonathan.

Fig. 14.

N ne-y o d Jonatha n runed.

Fig. 13.

Nine-year old Jonathan unprunec

Fig. 16.

The base of an aged Jonathan.

Fig. 15.

The Jona han tree in foliage.

Rome Beauty.—This is a somewhat difficult apple to bring into bearing and keep healthy and vigorous. In its young stages it is very vigorous and readily takes woolly aphis badly, while as it reaches its seventh or eighth year it is likely to stunt unless well fed and stimulated. Stable manure is the best fertiliser to apply, and under proper treatment the Rome Beauty is as productive as the Jonathan. It is inclined to be upright and close. The young tree must not be forked at its first pruning but at the second, cutting well above an outside bud or, wherever possible, to an outside lateral ; this opens the tree out. Care is required in forming the tree and bringing it into bearing. The short laterals should not be touched but the longer ones should be both winter and summer

Fig. 17.
Portion of aged Jonathan.

pruned. By judicious summer treatment of the laterals they are made to spur readily. The summer spurring should be done about the end of February or beginning of March. The Rome Beauty does not spur like the Jonathan when the laterals are left unshortened, but only bear fruit as a rule on the extremities. Figures 18 and 19 show a five-year old tree unpruned and pruned. It will be seen how the tree has been opened out by using the outside lateral growth for leaders. Care must be taken never to allow the tree to become stunted or lose vigour from any cause either of over-bearing or lack of nutriment or cultivation. Figure 20 shows a portion of an aged Rome Beauty in fruit.

30

Fig. 19.

Five-year Rome Beauty pruned.

Fig. 18.

Five-year Rome Beauty unpruned.

Granny Smith.—A first class New South Wales seedling and a variety well worth growing for long storing or export. The tree bears on the lateral well and on short spurs and should be treated in a similar manner to the Jonathan. It is a strong grower and, after it reaches five years of age, if the growth is in excess, the leaders may be let go for a season, care being taken to bring them back one half the following winter. Figures 21 and 22 show a five-year old tree unpruned and pruned.

Note.—Whenever the leaders of trees are allowed to go unpruned they should always be brought back one-third to one-half according to their strength and length the following winter ; also the leaders should be thinned out, only those required permanently being left unpruned, all others being removed, otherwise the

Fig. 20.
Some limbs of an aged Rome Beauty.

tree is too crowded, and not only the permanent leaders are weakened but also the lateral and spur growth is not developed properly. Figures 58 and 59 illustrate how this should be done.

Cleopatra.—This is a strong, hardy grower. It should be planted on the higher drier land owing to its liability to " Bitter pit." The tree is inclined to be upright and should be forced well open during the first few years, pruning so as to admit plenty of air and light. The Cleopatra is inclined to overbear and to bear very young, and often stunts from this cause. Devote the first four years to getting a good, roomy, strong tree by pruning fairly hard both top and lateral growth. The leaders can then be left longer each pruning until the growth lessens ;

Fig. 22.
Five-year Granny Smith pruned.

Fig. 21.
Five-year Granny Smith unpruned.

Fig. 24.
Five-year Cleopatra pruned.

Fig. 23.
Five-year Cleopatra unpruned.

some fruit may be allowed at four years old, and at the fifth it can carry, if well grown, a payable crop. It should be encouraged to carry as much fruit as possible with all due regard to healthy top growth. A light crop and strong wood growth generally means that large soft fruit liable to " pit " will result. The tree bears on both lateral and spur growth, and some laterals should always be permitted to go unpruned and these should be shortened in when spurred ; these longer lateral spurs give protection to the tree and encourage fruit development. The tendency of lateral growth is to slightly check the sap flow and cause fruit development. Figure 23 shows a five year old Cleopatra, and Figure 24 shows the same tree pruned. Figure 25 shows a lateral which was left unpruned (it takes as a rule two years to develop the spurs on an unpruned Cleopatra lateral). This is a permanent lateral carrying spurs which are multiplying each year and is now seven years old. The Cleopatra responds well to summer pruning of the laterals. Figures 26 and 27 show a nine year old tree unpruned and pruned.

Yates.—This variety prefers a heavier clay subsoil than most varieties—a subsoil which retains the moisture right through the summer months, for it is a very late variety and makes its greatest fruit growth during the last month before picking. The fruit should not be picked until it assumes a dark red colour and

Fig. 25. .
A spurred Cleopatra lateral.

a greasy skin appearance, just as the leaves begin to fall. It should then be picked at once, for within two or three weeks after this period is reached the fruit begins to fall badly. It is the best cold store apple grown, and improves in flavour in cold store. Owing to its fine quality and long keeping it always commands a high price. I do not advise any grower to plant this variety largely unless prepared to irrigate. It is naturally a small apple and requires forcing by manure and water to grow commercially, for the fruit otherwise, as the tree ages, runs small in size.

The Yates is very unsatisfactory on the lateral and only a few laterals should be allowed up the leaders. It throws as a rule from three to five apples from each bud ; it should therefore be short spurred to two buds only, and these short spurs should be left at every bud from base to tip. The laterals should also be summer pruned but care should be taken not to cut them too short and thus deprive the tree of too much of its foliage. Most of these laterals must be cut closer back in the winter. The fruit should be thinned when the size of marbles. This is done by taking the centre apple between the thumb and forefinger and rolling it over, when the fruit will come away, leaving the stalk behind. As all the apples in the cluster joint at the one base, the stalk must on no account be removed, otherwise it loosens all the other apples, which are liable to fall badly. Only the centre apple of a cluster is removed, because, if any of the outside ring is taken away it causes all the others in the ring to fall, leaving only the centre apple. This means

Fig. 27.

The same ree pruned.

Fig. 26.

Nine year o d Cleopatra unpruned.

that the crop will be too heavily thinned. The centre apple has a very short stalk and the outside ring longer stalks. The centre fruit, therefore, if not removed causes the others to be pushed off as it fills out. Figures 28 shows a five year old tree summer pruned. It is not safe to remove more foliage than has been taken off this tree. It will be noticed how sturdy the growth is, and, as a result of proper treatment, the nice crop of fruit the tree is carrying. Figure 29 shows a six year old tree also summer pruned and carrying a fine crop. The fruit will be seen right to the extremities of last year's growth, due to early development of the spurs by summer pruning and proper feeding and cultivation. When a tree becomes as fruitful as this the grower should use great care and judgment and never allow the fruit to develop on the extremities of the leaders until they are sturdy enough to carry the weight. Figure 30 shows two rows of aged trees

Fig. 28.
Five year old Yates Summer pruned.

carrying a very heavy crop of fruit. The fruit on these trees was not thinned out, and it will be seen how wasteful Nature is if left to do this work herself. The centre apples in many of these clusters will be the only ones remaining at harvest time. Figure 31 shows some limbs of Yates properly short spurred, and also shows how the fruit should be thinned. Where three apples are shown in the illustration a centre apple has been removed. Figure 32 shows a row of aged Yates properly summer pruned.

In all these illustrations it will be noticed that although the trees are carrying fine crops ample nourishment has been supplied to ensure sufficient growth on the extremities of the leaders for a thoroughly vigorous sap flow throughout the tree.

As the trees age the spurs increase and multiply as shown in Figure 33. There are seven developed buds in this cluster and a number just developing. It will be readily seen how impossible it would be for this spur to carry all the fruit which will set. The spur must therefore be thinned out where marked (a) leaving only about three frui.-buds as wide apart as possible.

Dougherty (wrongly called improved Yates in Western Australia).—This is another valuable cold store apple doing exceedingly well in Western Australia, where cultivated and treated properly. It requires the same treatment and

Fig. 29.
Six year Yates Summer pruned.

conditions as the Yates. Figure 34 shows some limbs of this variety, and Figure 35 shows a tree carrying a heavy crop of fruit. Such close attention to the thinning of the fruit is not so necessary as is the case with the Yates, and the laterals can be left longer. Figure 36 shows how this tree will overbear if not given proper attention and thinning to the spur growth and fruit.

. *Chandler's Statesman*.—This is a valuable late variety doing exceedingly well in Western Australia and a first-class cold store apple. It should be close spurred, only some laterals being left long. The tree is a very vigorous grower and, when the required formation and necessary leaders (about 15 to 18) have been obtained,

Fig. 30.
Two rows of aged Yates.

Fig. 31.
Some limbs of Yates properly pruned and thinned.

:uned and thinned.

Fig. 34.
Some limbs of Dougherty.

Fig. 32.
Aged Yates Summer pruned.

40

the permanent leaders can be allowed to go unpruned for a season but they must be shortened back again the following winter. They spur readily under this treatment and bear heavily. Figure 37 shows a tree carrying a heavy crop of fruit and yet making good top growth. Figure 38 shows a portion of a tree heavily laden showing even distribution of fruit. Figure 39 shows rows of this variety illustrating every tree doing its duty and carrying its load without any breaking down of the limbs. It will be seen by running the eye along these rows that although every tree is carrying up to its full capacity the leaders have made good top growth ensuring that the sap will be drawn to the extremities to nourish all fruit and spur growth and ensure a healthy sap flow throughout the tree to keep it thoroughly healthy and vigorous. Figure 40 shows a limb, giving some idea of how the tree carries its fruit. This variety stands storm and wind conditions without casting its fruit. It has proved a regular bearer in Western Australia.

. *Delicious.*—An American apple of great promise which has done remarkably well in Victoria and exports well. It is inclined to be large and requires heavy cropping to keep it down to size. The fruit is of good colour and rich aromatic flavour. The tree is a very heavy bearer and a strong vigorous grower which does not spur too well on the lateral except in light soils, but some laterals must be left long for protection. Figure 41 shows a limb of this variety. The tree

Fig. 33.
Thinning Yates spur.

can be thrown into bearing if very vigorous by letting the leaders go unpruned for a season as for Statesman.

Stayman's Winesap.—A famous American apple, doing well in Victoria, where it has been growing for some years. The fruit cold stores well, and is of fine colour and quality. Figures 42 and 43 show portions of trees of this variety. The fruit bears on both the lateral and short spur growth.

Black Ben Davis.—Another American variety grown in Victoria but not proved successful; owing to its having a very tender skin it is not able to stand the Bordeaux spraying for spot. It is a heavy cropper and a good quality apple. Figure 44 shows a limb of this variety.

Senator.—Another fine American variety in bearing in Victoria ; a good cropper, fruit a fine colour, shape, size, and flavour ; promises to be a welcome addition to our export varieties. Figure 45 shows a limb of this variety pruned in the same manner as for Winesap.

Rokewood.—A well known late apple and long keeper, does well in Western Australia. This tree is inclined to overbear and stunt. The tree should be well fed and encouraged to bear as much fruit as possible without checking its growth, the object being to grow the fruit from 2¼ to 2½ inches in diameter, as fruit over 2½in. in size does not keep well. The tree is a natural spurrer and only a few long laterals should be permitted, all others being shortened in close. Figure 46 shows a limb of this variety.

Fig. 36.
A imb of Dougherty too heavily aden.

Fig. 35.
Dougherty Appe.

42

Fig. 38.

Portion of Chandler's Statesman showing fruit.

Fig. 37.

Aged Chandler's carrying heavy φ.

43

Fig. 39.
Statesman carrying heavy crop.

Fig. 39.
Statesman carrying a heavy crop.

Fig. 41.
A limb of Delicious.

Fig. 40.
Showing a limb of Statesman.

Fig. 43.
Portion of Stayman's Winesap, showing distribution of fruit.

Fig. 42.
Stayman's Winesap.

Fig. 44a.
Showing a limb of Commerce.

Fig. 44.
Showing a limb of Back Ben Davis (leaves removed).

Fig. 44b.
Showing a limb of Champion.

Fig. 45.
Showing a limb of Senator.

London Pippin or Five Crown.—A well known variety, a heavy bearer and fine export variety under proper treatment. It has a very bad reputation for irregular bearing, often going several years without setting its fruit, but the writer has been very successful with it both in New South Wales and Victoria. Figures 47 and 48 show a five year old tree unpruned and pruned. Figure 49 shows an aged tree in flower. Figure 50 shows some limbs heavily laden (the leaves removed to show the fruit). This tree carried 31 cases of fruit. Figure 51 shows the base of an aged tree showing how productive the base can be maintained by proper treatment. The Five Crown is a natural spurrer—it is therefore necessary to close spur leaving only some laterals for protection and foliage, and checking

Fig. 46.
Showing a limb of Rokewood.

of the sap flow. The spurs must be thinned as they increase and multiply when the tree ages. The writer exported 750 cases of this variety in 1910 as early as the first week in February, per the s.s. " Summerset," the fruit bringing 12s. 6d. per case in London.

Sturmer Pippin.—Another well known variety much grown in Victoria and Tasmania. In the latter State it is their leading variety. The fruit brings poor prices even for export, but this variety is a consistent and heavy bearer and pays well. It is a natural spurrer but some laterals should be left long pruned. Figures 52 and 53 show a five year old tree unpruned and pruned. Figure 54 shows a limb of this tree (the leaves removed to show the fruit). This tree carried 11

Fig. 48.
The same tree pruned.

Fig. 47.
F ve y ar old Fve Cr m.

Fig. 49.
Aged Five Crown in flower.

Fig. 50.
Showing limbs of Five Crown carrying fruit (leaves
removed).

cases for the past three years. Figure 55 shows an aged Sturmer, illustrating the correct method of pruning with strong leaders.

The spurs so increase and multiply in this variety as the tree ages that it is necessary to heavily thin them, otherwise they rob each other, the flowers become weak and sterile and the tree does not set its crop well.

Munro's Favourite or Dunn's Seedling.—Does particularly well in this State and is a first class apple both for the English and German markets and for cold storing. The tree is a strong vigorous grower, rather slow in coming into bearing but spurs well both on natural short spurs and on the lateral, which will develop spurs in two years if left unpruned. The lateral answers well to summer pruning. When

Fig. 51.
Showing the base of an aged Five Crown clothed with
fruit.

the tree reaches its fifth year the leader should be let go for a season and then brought back again the following season. If the laterals are left unpruned they must be shortened in as soon as the spurs develop. This variety, when the leaders are permitted to go unpruned, often bears fruit on the tips. The tips of the leaders therefore should be removed, or the fruit removed immediately it develops, otherwise the limbs will be permanently distorted by bending over. All varieties which have this habit of forming fruit on the tips, when the leaders are left unshortened, should be treated in this manner. Figures 56 and 57 show a four year old tree unpruned and pruned. Figure 58 shows a six year old Dunn's Seedling which was not headed back the previous winter, but the

Fig. 53.

Five year old Sturmer pruned.

Fig. 52.

Five year old Sturmer unpruned.

Fig. 55.
Aged Sturmer.

Fig. 54.
Showing limb foliage removed to show fruit.

Fig. 57.
Four year Munro pruned.

Fig. 56.
Four year Munro unpruned.

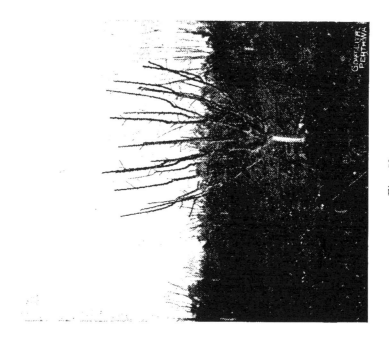

Fig. 59.
The same tree headed back.

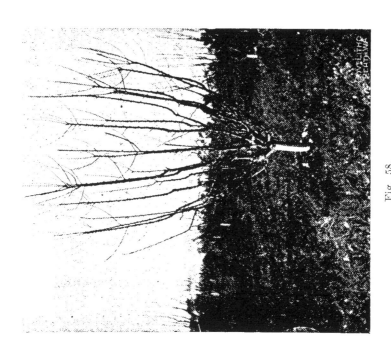

Fig. 58.
A six year old Dunn's Seedling not headed back.

leaders were thi....ed out and only those required to form the permanent leaders were left. This thinning out must always be attended to, otherwise the tree is checked by being too crowded, the permanent leaders are weakened, and the spur development interfered with. It will be seen how well clothed with short fruit spurs (as well as sufficient laterals to give protection and foliage) the leaders have become. Figu e 59 shows how this tree should be pruned. It will be noticed that the leaders have been shortened back about one-half, not only to

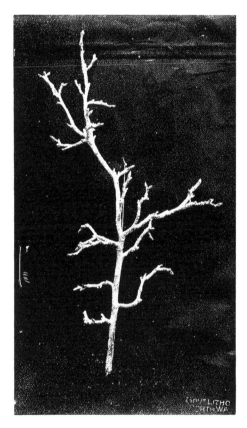

Fig. 60.
An old unpruned branched lateral.

strengthen them but also to prevent the tree becoming too high. It will be seen that these leaders have all been cut to fruit spurs, but in a vigorous tree the pruner need have no hesitation in pruning to a fruit spur for the terminal spur will force out into wood growth. The Dunn's Seedling is an upright grower, yet, owing to obtaining a wide base at the start, this tree is carrying 18 main leaders without crowding, for there is ample room be-tween each, and the tree has a hollow centre. The tree will also gradually open out as the crops become heavy up the leaders.

Should the tree still make heavy growth it will be necessary to again let these leaders go unpruned for a season, the heavy crops of fruit will then steady the growth.

The leaders in this tree must not again be forked or branched, for we have ample for the requirements of the tree. All the necessary leaders should be obtained in any variety of tree by the fifth season, and they must all be obtained before the leaders are allowed to run unpruned.

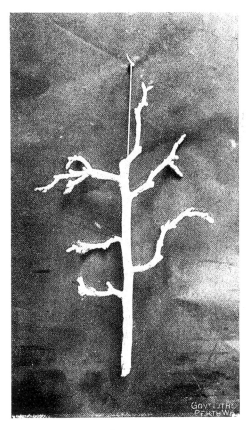

Fig. 61.
The same lateral pruned.

No greater mistake can be made than that practised by some growers of letting their trees go year after year unpruned, and this practice in the long run proves disastrous, for there are no main leaders, these having been lost amongst a lot of weak willowy top growth. The laterals can be left unpruned until they spur but they should then be shortenéd back not only to strengthen those spurs nearer the base, but also to prevent the tree from overbearing and producing undersized fruit. The length the lateral is to be left is dependent upon the vigorous state of the tree, the variety and the number of

58

spurs and amount of fruiting wood the tree contains. Figure 60 illustrates an old branched lateral of an aged apple tree which has never been pruned. There are far too many spurs and buds on thi; for the branch to nourish properly and mature the fruit, besides it is crowding up the tree too much. If this is not pruned back those spurs nearest the base will become so weak and exhausted that they will either fail to produce fruit or else die out. Figure 61 illustrates how this lateral branch should be treated. When the leaders have been allowed to go unpruned they should be shortened back the following winter as illustrated in Figures 58 and 59, and only in rare instances should they be allowed to go unpruned for a longer term. It is far better to bring them back, and if they still make strong growth let them go unpruned for a second time. The Jonathan

Fig. 62.
Unpruned trees—a wreck.

leaders must never be treated in this manner but always shortened back each winter. Figure 62 shows a fine crop brought about by not pruning but the trees are absolutely ruined.

As the trees age the spurs increase and multiply and they must then be thinned out, leaving about three fruit-buds as far apart as possible, otherwise, as stated before, they rob each other, and although the tree flowers heavily the setting of the fruit will not be satisfactory owing to the weakness and non-pevelopment of the buds, and if they do set their fruit, the spur is not strong enough to mature so many fruit, and small fruit of poor quality and flavour results. Apart from this there is, as a rule, not sufficient foliage on many varieties either for protection or for the assimilation purposes.

purposes.

Figure 63 shows an old fruit spur which has divided and multiplied as the tree aged. Owing to want of proper thinning it has become far too crowded. These spurs are to be found on both the aged apple and the pear. It should be heavily thinned where marked, if the tree contains many of them.

Fig. 63.
Aged fruit spur, should be pruned where marked.

🜨 🜨 🜨 🜨

The Pear.

The pear requires the same low, open, stout framework as is needed by other varieties of fruit.

For economical working conditions it is most important that no centre leaders be permitted, because these if left will take the sap and race away. Most pears naturally assume an upright, pyramid form of growth. Not only will such leaders take all the growth, but, on account of the resulting starvation of the outside ones, it is not possible to obtain a sufficient number of leaders for the tree to carry its fruit upon. The centre leaders, being few, and very rank in growth, do not spur readily, and the effect is that the fruit, being grown on the extremities and the tops of the trees, breaks them down or distorts them. Figure 64 illustrates this form of tree, and it represents a fair average specimen of many trees to be seen in certain districts of this State. Growers are far too timid about pruning the pear hard in its early years, and throwing it well open at the base. Growers who allow their trees to grow in this manner complain that, as the result of hard pruning, the tree grows ranker than ever ; and of course the trees will do this as long as orchardists persist in growing the trees in this manner ; but if the trees are pruned in a proper manner, with wide base and at least 15 to 18 leaders, the growth will be thrown, equally divided, into those leaders arranged and spaced equally round an open centre. If very vigorous, these leaders (which should be obtained by the fifth year) can be checked, and the tree can be brought into bearing by allowing the permanent leaders to go unpruned for a season and thereupon bringing them ᴗᴗck again, as illustrated for apples. Under this system they spur readily. Figure 65 shows a Williams grown in the manner described above. All the growth has gone to the centre of the tree, which is so crowded up that the fruiting-wood has not developed ; what there is, is weak, and the lateral growth also is weak and poor. The only way to treat this specimen is to remove the centre altogether, thin out the tree right through, and let light and air well into and round and about the leaders, to develop fruiting spurs and ripen lateral growth, as illustrated in Figure 66, showing the same tree pruned. This tree, by reason of the removal of so much timber, will make very strong growth

Fig. 64.
Badly trained Pear.

on the weaker leaders left, and this is what is required ; the more growth the better for the future of the tree. Next winter this tree should be pruned in the ordinary way, thinning out the top so as only to retain the permanent leaders required. These permanent leaders are then allowed to go unpruned for a season, and brought back again the following winter. The lateral growth will also be heavy, and this must be both winter and summer-pruned.

Some varieties of pears have a rank, spreading habit of growth, and if they are not treated with great care and attention during the first few years a very unsightly and unsatisfactory tree results. Wind knocks the tree about, limbs

Wind knocks the tree about, limbs

Fig. 65.
Badly trained Williams.

Fig. 66.
The same tree pruned.

are badly· broken and distorted, and fruit is badly marked and injured by the limbs coming in contact with each other

The¯pear is treated in pruning, for the first three years, much as illustrated for other fruit, and pruned hard to obtain wide, stocky, main and sub-arms. These latter should be subdivided and forked until from 15 to 18 main leaders have been obtained ; and it should be possible to obtain all the necessary leaders by the fifth year from the time of planting.

Each variety should be carefully studied, for there are great differences in the growth of many varieties, and the pruner must use great care and judgment in training each variety to the required form, and also exercise care in treating the spur-growth, for some trees will spur naturally on the short laterals if these are left, while others take years of winter pruning to develop fruiting spurs upon the laterals. · These latter can be quickly converted into fruiting laterals by both summer and winter-pruning of the laterals.

Williams Bon Chretien or Bartlett.—This is a very easy pear to prune, provided a good start is made, for it naturally runs up. A good wide base is required to build upon. When planting, remove the centre and throw the tree into wide, well-placed laterals. In the first pruning, again throw the tree wide, and prune hard, about six to nine inches being left, and cut out all laterals on the inside ; thin and shorten in those on the outside of the main arms, leaving only a few. The second year, prune hard, to leave about nine to 12 inches, and obtain a well-placed fork on each of last year's arms, if possible. This can often be attained by using an outside lateral to form a fork, and ultimately a leader. Trees can often be widened by utilising these laterals in the early stages of the tree's growth, and the necessary number of leaders can often be quickly obtained. The earlier you can obtain a number of leaders, the better, for the strong growth which the pear makes can be spread over a number of sub-arms, and by this means, together with widening the base, the tree's tendency to run to the centre is checked or negatived, and a more even development of tree and leaders is obtained. As before stated, all necessary leaders should be got by the fifth season. Thin out the lateral growth and shorten in that required, since bare limbs must not be permitted. In the third year prune from one foot to 18 inches, again obtaining a well-placed fork on each of the previous year's arms. if possible, and have plenty of room, for the base must not be crowded. We should now have at least eight leaders. Shorten in and thin the lateral growth. The fourth year prune a little longer, leaving about two feet, according to growth and stoutness of the tree, again getting a fork wherever possible, and required, on each of last year's arms ; and keep all laterals cut back and thinned. The lateral growth should be both summer and winter-pruned, short spurs or laterals always being left alone. Figures 67 and 68 show a four-year Williams unpruned and pruned. It will be noticed how badly this tree was pruned in its early stages ; the base is all cramped up. The tree was two years old when I took it in hand. By throwing out the sub-arms and utilising outside laterals for future leaders a fairly shapely tree has been secured, but the narrow base is a very serious fault, and although this can be rectified in the manner shown, yet the tree obtains some height before the needful width is gained. The tree has 17 leaders, and it will be seen that these are now left fairly long. The short laterals have not been touched, but all the longer ones have been shortened hard back, and will be again pruned in the summer—about the beginning of March. Keep the tree well-balanced, and do not have more leaders on one side than on another, but space them well all round the hollow centre, so that light and air can penetrate round and about each leader. Figure 69 shows an aged tree built up in this manner. The tree in question has a nice roomy base, giving a wide ·open tree with plenty of room for the 18 leaders it carries. These leaders are well-placed, and the tree is well-balanced and shapely ; the leaders are sturdy and carry ᶠruiting-wood

Fig. 68.

The same tree pruned.

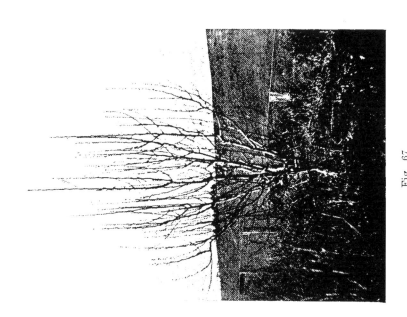

Fig. 67.

A five year old Williams Bon Chretien.

evenly distributed throughout ; and the base, although the tree is an aged one, is well furnished with fruiting-wood, which has been kept healthy by thoroughly nourishing the tree and permitting ample light and free air-circulation everywhere. As soon as the tree settles into bearing habits, the leaders should be hard pruned back, to keep down the height of the tree and to encourage good top-growth, which ensures the sap going to the extremities, thus feeding and nourishing all fruit as well as the spur and bud growth for the following season. The points of the leaders must be kept clear, so as to ensure a clean get-away of the top shoot in the same manner as for apples.

Fig. 69.
Aged Williams Pear pruned.

Kieffer's Hybrid.—A very erect grower, and a very unsatisfactory cropper unless planted alongside another variety flowering at the same time, when it will bear heavy crops. It should be formed with as wide a base as possible and pruned as for Williams, but some growers in the fifth year let the leaders go unpruned, and bend them over by tying them down with light binding-wire from near the extremities of the leaders down to a band placed round the trunk, taking care not to break them when bending. It should be done before the leaders become too rigid. This will cause the lateral growth to be thrown out strongly all along the length of the leaders. Two of these laterals suitably placed, one in towards the centre and one well out on each of the leaders bent down are then selected to make future leaders. The balance of the laterals are both summer and winter pruned close back and thinned out where excessive. This must be done each season until they spur. Those laterals selected for future leaders are pruned back each winter in the ordinary manner so as to keep them strong, treating them just as ordinary leaders. As soon as the tree settles into bearing, the old leaders bent down (the wire should be removed as soon as the leaders become fixed in their tied position) can be cut off flush with the outside new leaders selected from the

Fig. 70.
A row of Kieffer's Hybrid Pears pruned and in flower.

lateral growth which will now have become strong and of good height. This leaves the tree very shapely, open and sturdy, as shown in Figure 70, a row of aged Kieffer's pruned and in flower from base to tip. It will be seen that the leaders were allowed to go unpruned the previous season and they have now been cut hard back, spurs have been developed along their full length from every bud. These new spurs will bear a heavy crop, as shown in Figure 71, the same row of trees the following summer. The leaders it will be noticed are cut to flower buds, but in a vigorous tree these terminal flower buds will throw a strong wood shoot so that the pruner need have no hesitation in pruning to such buds.

Fig. 71.
The same row in fruit.

Fig. 72.
Showing the quantity of fruit on these leaders.

Although these trees are carrying very heavy crops they have made good healthy top growth ensuring a good sap flow. Figure 72 illustrates the quantity of fruit these leaders are carrying, while Figure 73 shows the quantity on the older portion of one of the leaders. This method causes some inconvenience in cultivation, etc.; until the old leaders are cut back, but it gives very satisfactory results if properly carried out. If this system is not followed, just as good results can be obtained by following the ordinary methods of pruning. The main arms must be thrown as wide as possible in the first few years' pruning, taking advantage of every outside lateral suitable for throwing out the tree and increasing the number of leaders. The leaders, as soon as they are strong enough, and as soon as sufficient

Fig. 73.
Showing a limb of Kieffer's heavily laden.

have been obtained, should not be headed back but allowed to go unpruned. This can generally be done by the fifth year. They must be brought back again the following winter to strengthen them, repeating this process if necessary until fruit-ing habits are formed. The laterals should be both summer and winter pruned to encourage fruiting spurs to develop, otherwise it takes years to develop them.

L'Inconnue, Beurre Capiaumont, Gansells, Winter and Madam Coles, Jar-gonelle, Glou Morceau, Beurre Bosc, Josephine, Clapp's Favourite, Beurre Clair-geau, and others can all be formed with a wide base and built up in the same manner, but special attention must be given to the manner in which they carry their spurs, for many of these varieties can be made to carry their fruit on the laterals. No

68

hard-and-fast rule can be laid down, for varieties differ in this respect owing to climatic and soil conditions ; only observation can demonstrate this, and growers should watch and experiment with the laterals for themselves ; by doing this they can work with Nature in place of forcing her unnaturally. It generally takes more than one season to develop spurs on pear laterals. There are always some of the shorter laterals which have never been cut back in previous seasons which will give some clue as to how to treat the lateral growth. When pruning Gansells and Vicars in one district this season (1912) I noticed well spurred two year old laterals. These points must be watched for. In such cases the laterals should not be shortened too severely either in winter or summer pruning, and in some cases are better left unpruned for a season or two. Figures 74 and 75 show seven-year old trees of Winter Coles and Bailey's Bergamotte varieties, while Figure 76 shows an aged Beurre Capiaumont pruned and in flower. This tree was started

Fig. 74.
Winter Coles.

with a very narrow base, but it was thrown wide in subsequent prunings and is now a very shapely, roomy tree carrying its 17 leaders without crowding. It is well clothed with fruiting spurs from base to tip. These spurs have been kept thinned out.

Pears of the Winter Nelis type, Figure 77, a seven-year old tree, are very difficult to prune to shape in their early stages owing to their unshapely manner of growth. Some growers prefer to let such trees go unpruned and shape them later when they commence to bear, but much growth is lost by doing this, and the tree is then even still more difficult to shape, and apart from this the tree becomes a wilderness without main leaders. Shape such trees as for other varieties for the first four years, choosing well placed shoots for future arms and sub-arms. Those which go out too wide, cut well above a top or inside bud, or, better still, to an upward lateral, and those

Fig. 76.

Aged eurnB Capiaumont pruned and in flower.

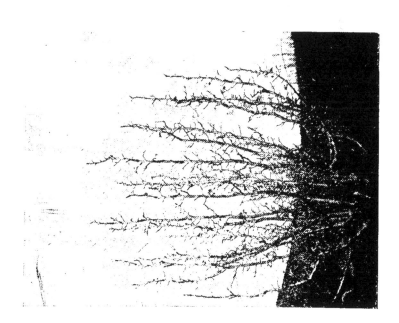

Fig. 75.

Bailey's Bergamotte

which grow too upright, cut well above an outside bud or to an outside lateral. Much good work can be done during the summer, for by judicious thinning and rubbing off of those shoots not required and pinching back others, a very shapely tree can be quickly made. After the third pruning it is best to prune fairly long if the tree is vigorous, but do not allow the leaders to become too willowy. In the young trees the limbs can be forced in the direction you wish them to go by forcing forks apart or forcing leaders into or away from each other by inserting light pieces of wood between them. By giving a little extra attention both summer and winter during the first four years, this type of tree can be grown to very good shape.

Fig. 77.
Pears of the Winter Nelis type.

It is always advisable to plant different varieties of pears flowering at the same time alongside each other, so that the blossoms can be cross fertilised. This ensures a good setting of fruit. Pears must be well fed and cultivated to get the best results, for they are greedy feeders and it pays to irrigate them, for by doing so they will not only carry and mature heavy crops, but it enables them to mature wood and spurs for the following season. If the trees become exhausted from want of attention they bear very irregular crops.

🖾 🖾 🖾 🖾

The Apricot.

The apricot should be pruned with a short main stem, 12 to 15 inches high, and very sturdy, wide main and secondary arms. Owing to its brittle nature, apricot wood is very liable to split ; narrow forks should, therefore, be avoided for that reason, and also because they are more liable than wide forks are to gumming. The main arms should be well spaced, and started as for other varieties.

Fig. 79.

Fi re year Apricot pruned,

Fig. 78.

Five year Apricot unpruned.

If well cared for, the tree is a strong, wild grower, and for the first four years it should be both summer and winter pruned, pruning the leaders and thinning them, as well as the lateral growth. The summer treatment is permissible only when the trees are strong and vigorous ; but the lateral growth may be treated during every summer up to the fourth or fifth year. Summer pruning should not, as a rule, be practised after the tree has settled into good bearing habits and the wood-growth has steadied.

Summer pruning hastens the building-up of the tree and brings it into bearing earlier, as well as helping to form a sturdy, strong tree and to check the natural tendency of the apricot, when young, to grow wild and rampant.

Both the summer and the winter prunings should be fairly hard for the first three or four years, after which the leaders should be left longer. The tree is naturally prolific and early in its bearing ; if planted in suitable soil and situation, and well cared for, it bears a good crop in its fourth year. It throws out short laterals, which are the fruiting spurs, all round the main and secondary arms ; and light and air circulation are well provided by the wide system of pruning, which ensures the full ripening and development of the fruiting wood. By heading off during summer, the required number of leaders are quickly obtained, and it is not then desirable to have any further forks or branching. The summer pruning will develop plenty of fruiting laterals, but after the discontinuance of summer treatment the leaders should in the winter pruning be headed just above the cluster of small lateral growth usually to be found about half-way up the last season's growth. This causes the sap to be slightly checked, resulting in the buds below the cluster throwing out light laterals. With proper attention to this point, no bare wood will result along the leaders. As the top growth ceases, the pruning becomes much more severe, because it is then necessary to prune the leaders hard in order to encourage top growth, and the clusters referred to are not required for checking the sap-flow.

Figure 78 shows a five-year old apricot which has been both summer and winter pruned for the previous four years. It is now bearing heavy crops of fruit, and the summer treatment has ceased. Figure 79 shows the same tree pruned and Figure 80 the same tree in flower. It will be noticed that the leaders have been headed just above the cluster referred to previously ; this will cause the bare wood below to develop fruiting spurs, similarly to that seen on the previous year's wood below. Notice how well distributed the fruiting wood is from base upwards ; no bare limbs exist, yet there is no crowding of the fruiting wood, which is nicely spaced and distributed throughout the tree. The tree has 24 leaders, which have not been forked or branched for the last two seasons. The base of the tree is wide, the tree open and roomy, without any crowding, while the limbs are strong and the forks wide. Thus the tree is able to carry and mature a heavy load of fruit without fear of its breaking, or of its being knocked about by the wind. Although there are 24 leaders in this tree, air and light have free entry everywhere, even when the tree is in foliage, as will be seen on reference to Figure 80a, showing the same tree in foliage. The leaders will now be gradually shortened at each pruning, because every year the tree will make less and less top growth.

When pruning for fruiting wood, every care must be given to the thinning and shortening in of the longer laterals to from four to six buds, cutting just beyond fruit buds and to a wood bud ; otherwise the tree is liable to overbear and pro-duce small, unmarketable fruit ; and, apart from this, the spurs will be too long. The short laterals are best left alone until after bearing, when they should be cut back gradually, as they begin to branch. Water shoots, unless needed to fill a space caused by the breaking or removal of a limb, are best removed flush, but in

Fig. 80.
Five year Apricot in flower.

Fig. 80A.
Five year Apricot in foliage.

the case of old trees not too well clothed with fruiting wood on the main and secondary arms, the water shoots should be retained, and fully utilised by constant cutting or nipping back during the summer, before they get too strong and too long. By this means good fruiting wood can be produced along bare limbs, to replace that lost. If left alone, water shoots will take the sap and rob the rest of the limbs.

Figure 81 shows a lateral spur which should be shortened back. Figure 82 shows the result in the absence of shortening ; it will be observed that the old portion has become barren. The next course is to cut this back where marked " a " at the joint of the old and new growths. In all probability, there are still some dormant buds at the base. If it is necessary to retain the lateral, shorten the

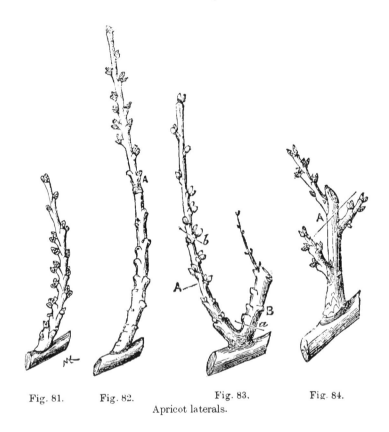

Fig. 81.　　Fig. 82.　　Fig. 83.　　Fig. 84.

Apricot laterals.

new growth back beyond a fruit-bud and to a wood-bud. It should, however, be cut back, as stated above, to force out new growth as illustrated in Figure 83, the old portion " B " is then removed at " a," when pruning in the following winter, and the new shoot " A " is pruned to a wood-bud at " b." After bearing the lateral, " a " will begin to branch as illustrated in Figure 84, and it should then be pruned as illustrated at " A."

By constant attention, the usefulness of lateral spurs can be maintained for long periods. Apricots in this State have reached the age of 60 years ; they are therefore, long-lived trees.

In many parts of Western Australia the apricot is a very unsatisfactory cropper, and this, in my opinion, is largely due to the long, dry summer ; after bearing, the tree is too exhausted to mature its spurs well. It often fails for several years running, which I attribute to the early failure of the soil-moisture, since cultivation is frequently neglected after harvesting, and, in consequence, the tree cannot mature its spurs and store up the necessary nutriment for the spring growth.

It is best to plant only in places where the trees can be watered, for the difficulty cannot be overcome except by intense cultivation. The tree should be watered just as the fruit begins to fill out, and again after the crop is harvested, to fill out and develop the spur and bud-growth and enable the tree to store up plant foods in its tissues.

Much can be done without water, in such cases by pruning the tree about March ; this strengthens the buds, and causes them to fill out. The leaders however, are best left alone until the winter-pruning. It is not advisable to remove too much foliage, for if any good is to result from the summer-pruning, sufficient foliage must be retained for the assimilation process, without which function the buds cannot be developed.

The apricot bears on young and old wood.

In lighter soils peach stock could be used to advantage in place of apricot stock ; while on heavy, wet soils, or on soil with a stiff clay subsoil, the plum stock, Myrabolan or cherry plum, will prove more suitable.

The apricot should be planted in well-drained soils in districts not subject to severe frosts at flowering time, or to late frosts, because the apricot is the first fruit to feel the effects of frost. Most other varieties of fruit will not even be affected by a frost which is severe enough to ruin the apricot crop.

The fruit should be well thinned when the trees set heavy crops.

☒ ☒ ☒ ☒

English Plums and Prunes.

These are practically the same varieties, for a prune is only a very sweet plum.

Some difficulty has been experienced in getting these plums to bear in Western Australia, but if the varieties are planted in close proximity so that the pollen will cross fertilise the blossoms, I think this difficulty will be largely overcome. Under proper soil and cultivation conditions many of these varieties make strong rank growth, and although they flower well they will not set their fruit. I had considerable trouble in New South Wales with these varieties, owing to the strong growth the trees made, and adapted the following method of pruning with great success, and this method may prove suitable in this State.

Any prunes and plums which make strong growth should be both summer and winter pruned up to the fourth year in the same manner as for apricots, that is, both the laterals and leaders should be pruned during the summer.

Start the trees off as for other varieties of deciduous fruits with low stem and open sturdy main and secondary arms and hollow centre, and prune regularly every winter and summer if the growth is strong, obtaining a nice, shapely tree as illustrated in Figure 85, a three year old tree pruned. It will be noticed that this tree (a Prune d'Agen) is an upright grower, and it has been necessary to throw the arms well out in this last pruning, and that no forks have been permitted so

Fig. 86.

Showing the pruning of a five year old Prune.

Fig. 85.

Three year o d Prune d'Agen tree pruned.

as to give ample room, for a greater number of leaders are necessary in these prunes and plums than in any other variety of fruit, because the foliage is scanty and the leaf very small, and unless a number of leaders are obtained the foliage is too scanty to protect the fruit and it is liable to sunscald on very hot days and especially during hot winds. Sun and light can, even with a large number of leaders, find free access and circulation, provided the tree is given a roomy base.

ᐧ ᐧ The small growth round the base and up the main arms should not be removed, but should be pruned every season. This shelters the main arms and trunk, and later on this small growth bears fine crops of fruit, which ripens later than the fruit above, and extends the harvesting. The fourth season the tree is still pruned

Fig. 87
Showing how the tree should be treated the following
winter.

fairly hard, and a fork obtained on each of the present leaders. After this the tree must be specially treated to get the best results. Figure 86 shows how the tree should be treated in the fifth winter's pruning ; the laterals and spurs are carefully pruned and thinned, and the leaders are thinned out, only leaving those required. These leaders should not be headed back, but left unpruned as shown in the illustration. This is an average specimen of a very large acreage treated in this manner. The small growth round the base, referred to before, will be seen in flower. It will also be noticed how evenly distributed the fruiting wood is throughout the tree. Although the tree shows splendid blossom, no fruit set, owing to the strong growth the tree was making. The following winter the tree

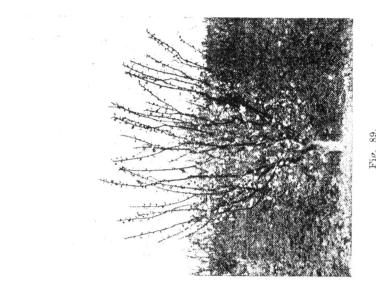

Fig. 89.

Showing the treatment the following winter again.

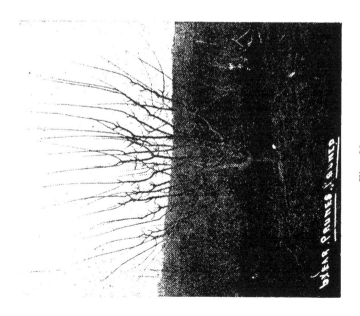

Fig. 88.

Showing the treatment the next winter.

79

should be thinned out, spur pruned, and the tops brought back one-half, say two feet being left, to strengthen them, as illustrated in Figure 87. The result of this treatment is to check the top growth of the tree and develop fruiting buds. It also causes fruit spurs to be thrown out at every bud along the full length of the leaders left unshortened the previous winter. These leaders it will be seen are cut back to fruit spurs, for all the buds are converted into spurs. The pruner need, however, have no hesitation in cutting to fruit spurs for the tree is so vigorous that the terminal buds will force into wood-growth and continue the leaders. These trees set some fruit, but as the growth was still heavy the leaders had to be allowed to go unpruned a second time. Figure 88 shows the seven year old tree pruned, with the leaders unshortened. The strong top growth will be noticed in this

Fig. 90.
Showing the tree in full bearing.

illustration, and Figure 89 shows the tree in its eighth year pruned, and the leaders again brought back about one-half. It will be noticed how well clothed with spurs this tree has become ; also note the number and closeness of the leaders, but as stated before it is not advisable to have too few leaders on these varieties. These trees now bore heavy crops of plums and the excessive top growth ceased. Figure 90 shows a nine year old tree in flower. After five years of this treatment the tree is now bearing heavy and regular crops of fruit. The tree now requires little pruning, but must be run over every winter, shortening the leaders back to a few buds and keeping them intact as for other trees. No forking or branching must be permitted after the necessary number has been obtained. The fruit is borne on spurs of one year's wood and upwards. The lateral spurs must be kept thinned and shortened back where required, for they branch and multiply, and they must not be allowed to become crowded, but kept strong and productive.

Summer Treatment.

Owing to the strong growth some of these plums and prunes make both of top and lateral (as illustrated in Figure 91, eight year old trees on the 1st December), it is sometimes necessary to do some summer pruning even at this age. These trees should be pruned about Christmas time, cutting back and thinning the laterals and thinning out the tops. Figure 92 shows these trees so treated, the following winter ; the leaders are permitted to go unpruned until the second winter, or, if desired, they can be headed back during the summer, about December.

The following illustrations show the system of summer pruning (which gives. identically the same result as the winter treatment). Figure 93 shows a five year old tree on the 1st December ; Figure 94 shows the same tree summer pruned.

Fig. 91.
Showing eight year old Prunes requiring summer pruning.

the leaders have been thinned out and the laterals cut close back. This tree was thinned and the lateral spurs run over only during the winter, the leaders being untouched until the following 1st December, when they were headed back as illustrated in Figure 95. By that date all the spurs had developed along the leaders as shown in the illustration. Figure 96 shows this tree when the foliage fell in the winter ; the spurs had developed well all up the leaders, and a comparison made with Figure 97, a tree treated by the winter system of pruning, already illustrated will show identically the same results obtained by the summer system of pruning. This tree only requires the short top growth cut back and the laterals run over in the winter.

Some plums, such as the Golden, Silver, and Sugar prunes may not require this treatment, because they are not, as a rule, rampant growers. The lateral growth should be left longer and encouraged to branch. These varieties as a rule should not be summer pruned.

The prune, to grow successfully, should be irrigated in this climate. The trees do not prove profitable if moisture fails, they drop their fruit badly, and it is small and undersized.

Wickson and Kelsey.—These are upright growers and the trees must be forced open by throwing the leaders into an outside lateral, and by utilising the outside laterals to obtain a fork or an additional leader.   In this way the tree can, in a few years, be made fairly open and shapely.   In these, as in other trees, an open centre must be kept.   Figure 98 shows two rows of Wicksons, and Figure 99 shows the same trees pruned.   All the lateral spurs must ·be shortened

Fig. 92.
The same trees the following winter.

and thinned because all the Japanese plums are inclined to over-bear. Figure 100 shows one of these trees in flower, showing the even distribution of fruiting wood.   The Wickson is a first-class export plum.   It can be picked three weeks before it is ripe as it both ripens and colours well off the tree.   Figure 101 shows a young Shiro Japanese plum carrying fruit. This is a nice, open sturdy tree carrying its fruit well round the base. Figure 102 shows this tree pruned the following winter.   The tree is a wide-spreading grower like the Burbank and Satsuma and others.   These trees should be carefully pruned and shaped in their early stages and every care taken to prevent them growing wild and straggly.   It is best to prune them fairly hard during the first few years to get a shapely tree, throwing the tree well up by pruning to inside buds, or utilising upward laterals if the limbs are growing wide and low. Every effort should be made to throw the tree well up and prevent limbs from growing across each other.   The spurs must be well thinned and shortened, especially as the tree ages.

Fig. 93.

Showing a five and-a-half year old Prune on 1st December.

Fig. 94.

Showing the tree summer pruned.

mmer pruned.

Fig. 95.
Showing the tree headed back on the 1st December following.

Fig. 96.
Showing the tree when the foliage fell.

Fig. 97.
Tree treated by winter system.

Fig. 98.
Two rows of Wickson Plums.

Fig. 99.
The same Wickson's pruned.

Fig. 102.
Young Shiro P um pruned.

Fig. 100.
Sho ing one of these trees n flower.

The Quince.

The quince as a rule gets little attention in the way of pruning ; yet the tree responds to good treatment under the secateurs, producing a better and more even class of fruit. A good formation should be obtained, as for other deciduous trees, and the lateral growth thinned and shortened. The lateral growth, as a rule, is very rank, bunchy, and excessive, and summer pruning and thinning should be practised, though the leaders are best not pruned during the summer. The fruit is borne on short growth thrown out from the previous season's wood ; therefore care must be used not to cut away too much of the short spur growth.

ஞ ஞ ஞ ஞ

The Cherry.

Only very few portions of this State are suitable for cherry cultivation, and great care and judgment are needed in the choice of district, situation, soil, and varieties.

The cherry requires deep, free, well-drained soil, moist, but with no excess of water during either summer or winter. The trees are not satisfactory in a heavy, retentive, or wet subsoil ; they fail early and gum badly. High, alluvial, well-drained soil near water-courses, or the light loams with good, free subsoils on the lower hillsides, are most suitable ; but irrigation must be provided.

This fruit should be planted in the cooler districts, away from the coast. Some cherry trees on the Narrogin State Farm, planted on a sandy soil with free subsoil, are doing well, and the plantation at Cherrydale, Donnybrook, is now bearing well.

The varieties which so far have proved the best in this State are—Heart of Midlothian, St Margaret, Werder's Early Black, Early Purple Guigne, and Bijarreau Napoleon. However, I have no doubt that many of the Californian varieties will prove successful under proper conditions of soil and cultivation.

The cherry is a difficult tree to prune in this State, owing to liability to gum.

Most varieties are upright growers, and every effort must be made to spread the tree during the first few years and to obtain a sufficient number of leaders. For the first three years, prune very judiciously and spread the tree well, obtaining as wide forks as possible, for narrow forks gum badly. Figures 103 and 105 show three year old trees and Figures 104 and 106, the same trees pruned ; these trees are not again pruned during the winter. Avoid having three shoots coming from the one close base by removing the central one ; otherwise, as the barks come together the limbs will be apt to gum very badly indeed. It is best to obtain as many leaders as possible during the first three or four years, for after this period it is not advisable to prune again, but to allow the tree to go without any winter-pruning. Then the tree should be run over every summer, removing any cross-limbs or branches and shortening in any laterals which require attention All new lateral growth should be pinched back during the summer.

Wide growers should be encouraged to grow more upright, by pruning to inside buds or to upward laterals.

By judicious treatment during the first three years a shapely tree can be formed.

All big cuts should be painted over with white lead, and if it is necessary to remove big limbs this should be done in midsummer.

The tree should be watered just as the fruit begins to swell, and again immediately after the fruit has been harvested, to fill out and strengthen the fruiting-wood and buds for the following season. This is very necessary, owing to our long, dry summer. The cultivation must be kept up and be very thorough and deep right up till the autumn rains fall.

Fig. 103.
Three year old Cherry.

When the cherry trees are planted, cut them back as for other trees, removing the centre and retaining three well-placed laterals for the main arms. In the first winter-pruning, cut the leaders back to from eight inches to 12 inches. Do not, however, attempt to obtain forks on the upright growers, but throw the tree as wide as possible. In the case of a wide grower, obtain forks if it is possible and if there is room.

In the second and third prunings cut back to from 12 inches to 18 inches according to growth, and obtain a fork on each of last season's leaders, using a lateral if necessary, to obtain a fork, and spreading the upright growers as wide as possible.

All lateral growth should be pinched back during the summer. Any growth starting from the main stem during the first season is also best pinched back instead of being removed altogether, because of the foliage obtained by pinching back. This growth affords protection from the sun; and in this climate it is very necessary to shield the trunk, main arms, secondary arms, and leaders from sunscald by giving the tree all the foliage possible. If the tree suffers from sunscald in any of its parts, there will be no possibility of preventing its gumming ; only in those trees which have a fine, green, healthy bark will gumming be avoided. Sunscald binds the bark to the cambium layer, closes the pores, and this interferes with

Fig. 104.
The same tree pruned.

the sap-flow. This interference with the sap-flow is largely the cause of the disease known as gumming.

In the fourth year the leaders should be pruned very long, (or if sufficient leaders have been obtained, as in illustrations, they are allowed to go unpruned) because the cherry in this State is highly impatient of the knife. It should now, therefore, be pruned as little as possible, and the leaders should be left from two feet to two and a-half feet, according to the vigour of the tree.

Give attention to the tree during the summer, for by constant nipping of the laterals and by the removal of cross and useless branches little remains to be done in the winter.

Fig. 106.
The same tree pruned.

Fig. 105.
Three year old Cheiry.

The Almond.

During the first few years almond trees. are pruned as for other deciduous trees, a well-shaped, open tree being obtained, with about 12 leaders. Weeping or spreading varieties should be encouraged to grow more upright, by pruning hard to an inside bud or an upward lateral if the branches go too wide or low-spreading. Upright varieties should be encouraged to spread by pruning well above an outside bud or to an outside lateral, the lateral of course being cut back slightly according to its strength and the length required.

Fig. 107.
Five year old Almond pruned.

The almond is inclined to throw a mass of laterals as well as a bunch of top growth from the extremities of the leaders cut the previous season. This bunch of leaders should be thinned out, leaving only two to form a fork, as wide as possible and the lateral growth should be thinned out, and those laterals which are retained should be shortened back.

For three years the pruning is fairly hard, but in the fourth year the leaders are left about 18 inches long, while at the fifth pruning the leaders are left from 2ft. to 2ft. 6in. long, pruning above the cluster of laterals to be found halfway up

Fig. 108.
Row of Almonds used for a breakwind.

Fig. 109.
Lauder's Almond.

these leaders as shown in Figure 107. This slightly checks the flow of sap, thus causing lateral spur growth to develop up these long leaders, which otherwise, owing to their length, would be inclined to remain bare of lateral spurs. This tree illustrates the form desired in an upright grower, and all the leaders needed have been obtained. The tree is five years old, from planting.

The almond bears on new and old spurs thrown out on both the lateral growth, which should be shortened back, and spurs thrown out on the main limbs and leaders. Short laterals can be left alone until they spur and branch ; they should then be pruned as required. Figure 108 shows a row of almonds in flower, five years old ; these trees are grown for a breakwind and are planted 12 feet apart ; they carry more leaders than is usually permitted, simply because they are intended for shelter to the orchard. However, they show the form of tree required. Almonds make a good breakwind planted in this manner round an orchard ; they also make handsome avenues, and, if cared for, they are very productive.

Figure 109 shows portion of a young almond raised by Mr. Lauder, of the Upper Chapman, where the nut is doing remarkably well. The varieties raised by Mr. Lauder are proving highly productive. The tree shown requires pruning and shaping, and the lateral growth should be shortened in as otherwise it will become largely barren, bearing only on the extremities.

A wide opening offers for the cultivation of the almond in Western Australia. The tree is a deep rooter, and requires deep, loamy soil. Thanks to its deep-rooting habit in suitable soil it will withstand drought conditions better than will most deciduous trees, provided the cultivation is thorough.

Ample phosphate, potash, and lime should be given to the almond, and mixed varieties should be planted to permit cross pollination.

🔯 🔯 🔯 🔯

The Peach and the Nectarine

No tree calls for more skilful treatment than does the peach, owing to the need for always having a supply of fresh wood and spur or lateral growth. The peach bears only on the last season's wood, and care must always be given to the proper feeding and cultivation, so as to ensure a vigorous growth.

The tree comes into bearing at a very early age, and it is wise to form a low, stocky tree, with a very strong, open framework, to carry the crop ; getting a wide, open base and a roomy top, with plenty of space in the centre and between each of the leaders.

Some pruners in this State practise far too open a system of pruning. This I condemn, for it leads to sunscald of the bark and checking of sap-flow. The centre should be roomy, but not wide open, and it should carry a double row of leaders right round ; with a wide base there is room for 18 to 20 leaders. Once the full number has been obtained, the leaders must be maintained intact, without branching, in the same manner as obtains with the apple and all other deciduous trees. If once these leaders are lost, the grower's control over his tree is also lost, for all the top-growth goes to fruit-buds and the lower fruit-bearing wood starves. By pruning hard and feeding well, the tree can be kept in good

94

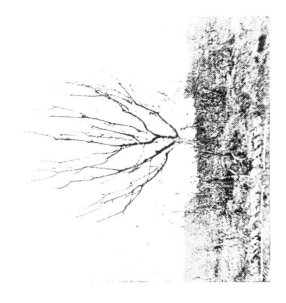

Fig. 111.
The same tree pruned.

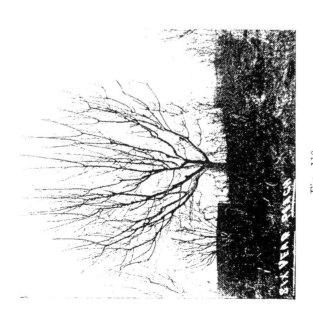

Fig. 110.
Shows a six year old Elberta Peach.

95

Fig. 112.
A Comet Peach pruned—wide forks.

Fig. 113.
Goldmine Nectarine pruned—wide forks.

bearing, from base to top, for 18 to 20 years, but it becomes necessary then to cut the tree hard back and start it afresh, as illustrated in the chapter, at the end of this work, on the renovation of trees (Figure 151). By hard pruning, and by keeping the tree roomy (for it must be remembered that the peach is a heavy-foliaged tree and will not stand crowding) the fruiting laterals all up the main and sub-arms can be kept healthy and productive, with a constant renewal of gr wth ; but if light and air are shut out by overcrowding of the top, the lower fruiting-wood soon becomes exhausted and starved, and bare, barren limbs result.

Figures 110 and 111 show an Elberta peach unpruned and pruned. The tree is grown on the upright narrow base system, and the figures are included for

Fig. 114.
Tree correctly pruned this season, but in the past has been allowed to spread too much.

the benefit of those who prefer to follow that system. Figures 112 and 113 show a Comet peach and a Goldmine nectarine grown on the wide base system, pruned, and just coming into flower.

I would urge the wide system, not only because it gives so much room, permitting of a greater number of leaders and therefore of more fruit, but also because it admits of a lower and much stronger tree. Anything that is gained through saving of labour in cultivation on the narrow-base system is lost again in picking the fruit and pruning, by reason of the height of the tree.

Figure 114 shows a peach which has been well pruned this season, but it has in the past been allowed to spread far too wide. The base is correct, but the leaders should have been grown more upright.

97

Fig. 116.
The same tree pruned.

Fig. 115.
A four year old peach unpruned.

98

Fig. 118.
The same Peach pruned.

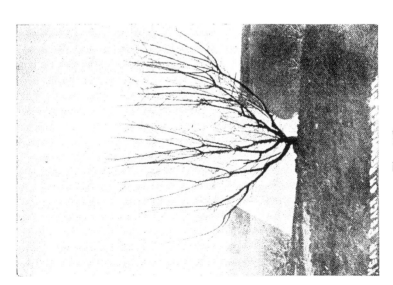

Fig. 117.
Five year Peach unpruned.

For the first three years prune hard ; nine inches the first year, 12 inches the second year, and 18 inches the third year to be left at each pruning. Remove the inside leader of the fork in the first pruning if necessary to open out the tree-base, or throw the leader into an outside lateral. This forms a very sturdy, open, well-spaced framework. Remove all excess of laterals and shorten in others in the second pruning to make some fruiting wood for the following season ; for a vigorous peach may be permitted to carry some fruit in its third season. At the third pruning the lateral growth is shortened, thinned, or removed, as may be required ; since the tree, if well grown, can carry a fair amount of fruit in its fourth season from

Fig. 119.
Showing the strength in this form of tree.

planting. In the fourth pruning the leaders are left longer, according to the vigour of the tree, from 2ft. to 2ft. 6in. being left. Figures 115 and 116 show a four-year Elberta unpruned and pruned. The tree is roomy, open, and the leaders well spaced and carries nice fruiting wood throughout. The lateral growth has been thinned, shortened or cut close back to two wood buds to form wood for the following season. Figures 117 and 118 show a five-year old tree unpruned and pruned, an ideal shaped tree, low butted, roomy, strong and carrying good fruiting wood from base to tip. Figu e 119 shows the great strength in this form of tree, although only five years old. The leaders have been left fairly long, but after this season the pruning will require to be hard to keep the tree vigorous, for it now carries heavy crops of fruit which will tend to check its vigour somewhat, and the vigour must be kept up to furnish a constant renewal of bearing wood. Although this tree looks roomy and open, Figure 120 shows it in foliage and gives some idea of how necessary it is to keep the leaders well apart. We now have a double row of l aders all round a roomy centre and these leaders must be kept intact right through the tree's existence without any branching. Figure 121 shows a six-year old tree in full bearing. It will be noticed that the leaders have not been branched and no forks have been permitted for the past two seasons and no branching must be permitted in future, otherwise the leaders will be lost. The points of the leaders must always be kept clear, but the small lateral growth immediately below the tips should not be removed, because these, by checking the sap flow slightly, causes the buds below to throw out fruiting laterals, and in this manner the buds are developed down below, and no bare wood results, such as is often seen in the peach. The strength in this six-year old tree is shown by the man sitting in a third season's fork ; the tree is open, roomy, and carries nice fruiting wood from base up, and the

Fig. 120.
Showing the tree in foliage.

tree carried a heavy crop both the previous and the following season. The tree is nine feet high to where pruned, and the fruit can be picked without the aid of a ladder. The leaders must now be hard pruned every season to keep them growing strong. Figure 122 shows an eight-year old peach tree badly pruned. A glance at Figure 121 will illustrate the difference in the two systems. In one the leaders are kept intact ; in the other the leaders have been lost and the top of the tree has all gone to fruiting wood, while the base is already barren and in two years' time the tree will only bear on the top, all the lower portion of the tree becoming barren (as shown in Figure 150, renovating peach). It will be noticed that in Figure 122 the top is a mass of fruiting wood and the reader has only to picture in his mind what this tree will be like when in foliage and how little chance it has of maintaining its lower fruiting wood healthy and productive. The only thing to do is to heavily thin out the top, regain the leaders, and permit sunlight . and air free entry and try to develop the lower fruiting wood again by severe shortening back. In pruning the peach for fruit,

Fig. 121.
Six year old Peach pruned, showing strength in limbs.

Fig. 122.
A badly pruned eight year old tree.

short woolly budded laterals or spurs may be left alone where not too crowded. Weak spurs should be shortened back to the two wood buds near the base. Where the fruiting and weak wood is too thick it may be necessary to remove some altogether, but always bear in mind that fruiting wood will be required for next season, as the peach and nectarine only bear on last season's growth. There is always a certain percentage of spurs die each year, and others become exhausted or too long and useless, and these must be replaced, or long bare limbs result. It is a good plan to always leave fruit buds in excess of what is required, because not one half of the flowers set fruit. The best fruit laterals are the strong shoots carrying two flower buds with a wood bud between. These should

Fig. 123.
Two unpruned Peach leaders.

be shortened back so as to only leave from four to eight of these cluster fruiting buds according to the carrying capacity of the tree, and the amount of fruiting wood available. In the early peaches the habit of throwing their flower buds just as the sap rises is very prevalent in this State. This undoubtedly can only be overcome by intense cultivation. I would advise nipping the lateral shoots during the summer, or pruning them immediately the fruit is harvested. This would have the effect of strengthening the buds, or else, leave the pruning until the pink of the blossom shows, for those buds which r.main up to that stage do not fall and there is no risk of cutting off the fruit when pruning. Then shorten back those which show an excess of blossom, leaving others entirely alone and

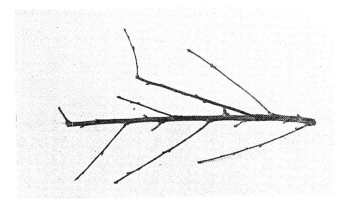

Fig. 125.
The same leader pruned.

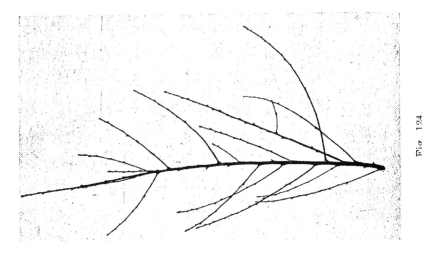

Fig. 124.
strong leader on a vigorous young Peach.

shortening others to wood buds to throw fruiting wood the foll wing seasons, for a constant renewal of growth must be maintained.   Figure 123 illustrates two peach leaders from young trees which were unpruned during the winter.   It will be   seen   that   far   more   fruit   has set than the limbs can possibly carry.   The result of this will be that not only will the fruit be small and unmarketable, but the future of the leaders has been seriously impaired, for very little growth will be made.   The   leaders   will   become   weak   and   willowy,   and the lateral growth barren, only bearing on the tip of fresh wood put out each season.

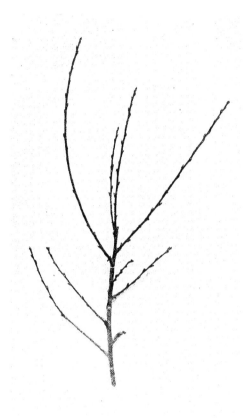

Fig. 126.
The extremity of an older Peach leader.

Figure 124 illustrates a strong leader on a vigorous young tree, while Figure 125 shows how this should be pruned.   Figure 126 illustrates the extremity of a leader from an older tree, while Figure 127 shows how this should be pruned.   The bunch of terminal growth has been removed, retaining the best placed and strongest shoot to continue the leader.   The extremities of the leaders must always be kept clear in this manner.   Peaches and nectarines should, wherever possible, be irrigated during the summer months in Western Australia.

The cultivation of these fruits, especially the early ones, is as a rule entirely neglected after the crop is harvested, and owing to the failure of soil moisture the development of the fruit spurs and the storing up of the plant foods mentioned in the early part of this book cannot take place, and when the rain does come in the late autumn very serious damage results to the tree and subsequent crop. The peach should be planted in good loamy soil.

Fig. 127.
The same leader pruned.

The Fig.

The fig requires little in the way of pruning. Only shape the tree when Nature does not do this herself, and cut back any leader which runs away from its fellows. The tree should be cut back to the required height in the nursery. If this has not been done, the young tree should be headed back to the required height when planting.

Keep the tree shapely by removing any cross limbs, and as the tree ages some thinning of the top growth becomes necessary ; but, in thinning, it is best to remove the growth flush from its parent stem in place of shortening only.

Some varieties sucker badly, and these suckers should be carefully removed by cutting off flush with the main roots or lower part of the trunk, whichever they may spring from.

🔄 🔄 🔄 ᴍ

The Olive.

The olive requires some pruning. It is best to remove the centre leader, for economical purposes, and grow the tree in the bush form, so that the gathering of the fruit can be more easily and cheaply done. The tree will grow to a great height if the centre leader is left.

The lateral growth may be thinned out, and the remainder shortened in lightly. The olive bears on the younger wood, the flowers coming on short, young growth thrown out from the younger wood. Therefore, it is very necessary that ample young wood be provided. If there are too many leaders, or if the tree is too dense or too compact, then the leaders should be thinned out, and those which are retained should be shortened back if making too much wood.

These measures will keep the tree as low as possible for picking ; but avoid cutting too hard, for this results in a very dense growth.

ᴍ 🔄 🔄 🔄

Walnuts and Chestnuts.

These trees require little pruning, as Nature generally herself shapes the tree, but for reasons of economy it is best to remove the centre leader. Figure 128 shows a walnut shaped by Nature. Should any leader get away from its fellows, it may be shortened back ; otherwise, let the tree alone, except in case of its becoming too crowded, or of too many arms coming out from the main stem, when they should be thinned out. All cross limbs should also be removed.

Fig. 128.
Walnut.

108

The Persimmon.

This tree needs some pruning, but care must be taken not to cut off too much of the fruiting wood. The fruit is borne on the short shoots thrown off the previous season's growth. The tree first requires shaping similarly as for other deciduous trees. It naturally forms a shapely tree, and after it is once formed the leaders should be kept fairly hard pruned to induce new growth, and the lateral growth should be kept thinned out, more especially as the tree ages. However, only the longer laterals should be cut back ; for, if all laterals are tipped, no fruit will result, since the fruit is, as a rule, borne on the terminals. Figure 129 shows a persimmon about seven years old unpruned, and Figure 130 shows the same tree pruned.

Fig. 129.
Persimmon.

Fig. 130.
The same tree pruned.

The Gooseberry.

These deciduous shrubs are best suited to the cooler districts with good soils and ample moisture. The plants can be obtained from cuttings about 15in. to 18in. long, from well-ripened, strong wood, the buds and prickles being removed from the lower end, as illustrated in Figure 131 (illustrations after Wright), or else by layering. When struck, the cuttings are planted out in rows about 5 feet apart, the rooted cuttings being about four feet apart in the rows.

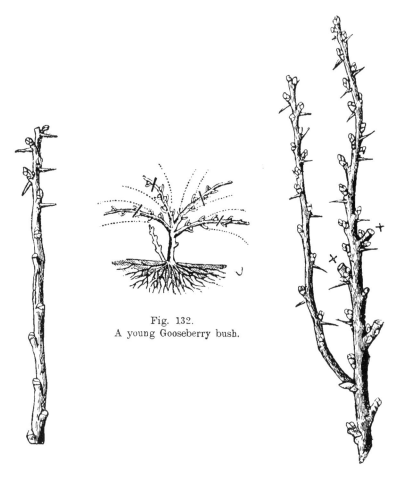

Fig. 132.
A young Gooseberry bush.

Fig. 131.   Fig. 133.
Gooseberry cutting.   Two and one year old wood..

The commercial varieties mostly grown in Australia are—

Red.	White.
Billy Dean	Whitesmith
Crown Bob	
Rifleman	
Roaring Lion	

The bushes should be systematically pruned, to obtain good-sized fruit and regular cropping. All suckers should be removed. The main stem should be raised well above the ground level before being allowed to branch—as a rule, about 12 inches is sufficient. Figure 132 illustrates a young bush marked where it should be pruned. These four limbs will branch in the following season as marked by the dotted lines. The season after, these new shoots are cut to good stout buds, leaving 12 inches if the growth is vigorous. The lateral shoots, which are not required, should be shortened close back.

The fruit is borne on two-year and older wood. Figure 133 illustrates two-year wood with a one-year shoot. Most of the laterals on this branch have been cut close back as at " x " ; this prevents the bush from becoming too dense and crowded. The young one-year shoot is left where there is room, so that the older wood can be removed. This practice keeps the bush highly productive. The older wood becomes worn-out and exhausted ; therefore a constant supply of new growth is required to replace exhausted wood, especially in the centre of the bush. Well-developed fruiting buds or spurs are shown all along the older wood. In the one-year shoot the buds shown will develop into fruiting spurs for the following season. Figure 134 shows bearing wood in fruit, two laterals left for future bearing wood, and two shortened back.

Fig. 134.
Bearing wood and laterals.

The Citrus.

The Orange and Mandarin.—On planting, the trees are cut back, Figure 135 showing a good healthy tree from the nursery and Figure 136 the same tree pruned, therefore they must be reshaped again at the first pruning, but much can be done by going over the trees during the summer, for by nipping or rubbing off shoots the growth can be directed into the required channels, and a shapely tree grown without any waste of energy or wood-growth. The stems of young citrus trees should always be protected from the sun and hot winds, and the strawsheaves from bottles split down and wrapped around the main stem are most suitable for this purpose.

Fig. 135.
A young Orange tree
from nursery.

Fig. 136.
Showing how the tree should
be pruned when planted.

The young tree will throw a mass of growth down the main stem, as well as at the top, and this growth should be either nipped back or rubbed off, leaving only those shoots required to form the future main arms of the tree. Choose three or, at the most four, well-placed shoots for this purpose, starting at different places on the main stem, the lowest of which should be 18 inches from the ground. The small growth up the main stem, if this is not protected, should not be rubbed off, but nipped back, because the leaves will afford protection to the unprotected main stem.

The same attention to permitting the free entry of air and light must be observed with the citrus family as with the deciduous trees if they are to be kept healthy, productive, and free from disease.

Very little pruning is required if the trees are properly attended to every year, and this pruning should not be done during the winter, but just before one of the several growths these trees make—just before the spring growth for preference. Figure 139 shows a good specimen of young orange. It is very desirable to grow all citrus in the bush form, and this object should be kept in view all the time.

The centre of the tree should never be allowed to become crowded ; keep the small growths in the centre well thinned out, so that light and air can penetrate freely throughout the trees ; keep the outside growth thinned out sufficiently

Fig. 137.
A three year old Orange.

to permit entry of light and air, and no more ; do not overdo the thinning. \ If the outside becomes too dense, the inside growth dies. Apart from this, a dense tree is far more liable to sickness and disease than a tree properly thinned.

Water shoots, if not required for leaders (and they must be well placed for this purpose) should be removed flush and never allowed to make headway, for they rob the rest of the tree of sap and check the general growth of the tree. If they are retained they must be headed back, otherwise, if they are allowed to run un-becked, a two-storied or badly balanced tree results.

Keep the tree well balanced. Cut back any lateral branches that are inclined to grow too far out to an upward lateral, and remove any which come down too close to the ground. Figures 138, 139, 139a show well-cared for orange trees at different ages. Figure 140 shows a young mandarin, and Figure 141 shows the same tree pruned ; the wind was unfortunately blowing strongly when the photo. was taken and the thinning does not show up as well as it otherwise would, but the centre has been thinned out and just sufficient of the dense outside growth removed to permit light and air free entry. The bottom growths touching the ground have also been removed. Figure 142 shows a well-grown seven year old mandarin in heavy bearing.

The lower growth on citrus must not be trimmed up too high, for it is very necessary that the trunk and main crown roots, which are just on the surface of the ground, should be protected. This growth is only removed sufficiently high

Fig. 138.
A good shaped young Orange tree.

to prevent the growth from coming to the ground when carrying fruit. As the tree ages it is necessary to keep removing the lower growth, or throwing it up by cutting to the upward laterals, because the tendency of the growth is to come downwards, owing to the heavy crops of weighty fruit the trees carry.

No dead wood must be permitted to remain in the tree either in the centre or tops, and care and attention must be given right through the tree's life not to allow it to form a compact mass of foliage.

The annual wood growth for fruit must be kept up by keeping the trees thoroughly healthy and in a growing state by thorough cultivation, manuring, and irrigation. If attention is given to allowing sufficient light and air, the trees will bear well and keep very free from disease. Figure 143 shows a nice limb of Valentia late . orange· Figures 144, 145, 146 show highly productive orange trees, which have been well pruned and cared for.

and cared for

The Lemon.—The lemon requires far more attention than the orange, owing to its rambling habit of growth, also because it does not so readily provide itself with fruiting wood. It should be grown into a good roomy, stocky tree or bush, with no central leader. Form the young tree, and treat it in every way as for the orange during the first few years. By pinching and cutting, the leaders can be kept from rambling in early life. Strong shoots must be cut flush away when not required, and all other laterals suppressed by nipping back. Figure 147 shows a well-shaped young lemon. As the tree ages keep the small growth in the centre

Fig. 139.
A good shaped young Orange tree.

well thinned out and that retained nipped back, and keep the outside growth from becoming too dense, to permit free circulation of air. All pruning should as a rule be done just before the spring growth, but if the tree is very vigorous, pruning about December will check the strong rank growth, and promote the lighter fruiting growth.

The aim of the pruner is to prevent wild growth and encourage small fruitin growth, without altogether suppressing the natural habit of the tree.

All cross limbs must be removed, and the leaders shortened back, otherwise they become long and wild, and the fruit is ruined by being thrashed about by the wind, or by the limbs coming down on top of each other, and spiking the fruit on the thorns. The lower growth must be kept trimmed up clear of the ground. Figure 148 shows a young lemon in bearing, a well shaped, open and roomy tree, about seven years old.

The lemon bears all the year round, and requires constant attention, not only in pruning but also by heavily manuring, liming, and constant and thorough cultivation. Owing to the constant picking, for the tree bears all the year round, the bush form is the most suitable class of tree to grow, and greatly lessens the expense of harvesting. By keeping the main leaders within bounds, and by continually nipping or cutting the lateral growth, a good supply of light fruiting wood is kept up. The lemon requires more light and air than the orange, because it bears well right through the centre of the tree, as well as on the outside, so no crowding must be permitted in any part of the tree.

Fig. 139a.
A well shaped Orange tree.

Fig. 141.
The same tree prun...

Fig. 140.
A young Mandarin.

Fig. 142.—A seven year Mandarin.

Fig. 145.

A productive and well pruned tree.

Fig. 144.

A well shaped and pruned Orange carrying a heavy crop.

Fig. 146.
A productive and well pruned tree.

Fig. 148.

A young Lemon n bearing.

Fig. 147.

A good shaped young Lemon tree.

The Loquat.

This tree, being an evergreen, does not call for the same attention in pruning as deciduous trees require. The main stem should be from 18 inches to two feet in height to first branch, if planted in the orchard, but if used for a break-wind the main stem should be from two feet to three feet in height.

The centre leader should be removed when the tree is planted and encourage a bu h habit of growth, but prevent the tree from spreading too much by judicious pruning, and removing of the side shoots. As the tree ages it is necessary to thin out by removing limbs or branches when too crowded. Keep the tree shapely, and not too crowded in any part. The pruning is best done just before the growth starts in the Autumn. The fruit is borne on branching spurs, which start out from the terminal buds in the late autumn, the flowers opening early in the winter, and the fruit ripening early in the spring. Fresh growth starts out from the base buds of these branching spurs which die back after bearing. This young growth is often too thick, and requires thinning, otherwise overcrowding results. The old decayed fruit-clusters remaining after bearing should be removed, as they encourage fungoid diseases, such as " Black Spot " of the loquat. As the fruit is produced in the damp weather of winter these diseases are liable to be transferred to the fruit.

⌦ ⌧ ⌦ ⌦

Renovating Old Trees.

The Peach.—Peach trees, whether old or young, that have become exhausted or run out and b:come unprofitable, bearing only on the extremities and top of the tree, due to bad pruning and cultivation in the young tree, or exhaustion, due to age in the old tree, can be given a fresh lease of life by heading right off as illustrated in Figure 149, and started off afresh. The trees can be done by degrees, a few each season, so that growers will not be deprived of all the fruit if required to carry on with. The tree should not be cut too far back because the old wood left will throw out new laterals from dormant buds all up the old limbs. On the other hand the tree must be cut back severely enough to ensure its starting strongly again, for if too much top is left only weak growth results. Figure 150 shows an unprofitable tree which pays to cut back. Figure 151 shows how this should be done ; any lateral growth down the limbs should not be touched. The tree will not always burst at the sawcuts, so any stubs must be removed in the following season's pruning. Figure 152 shows a tree twelve months after cutting back. It will be noticed what strong healthy growth it has made and how well clothed the old limbs have become with new lateral growth. The tree should be carefully pruned and thinned, choosing the best placed and strongest shoots for leaders and stubbing others back. Do not take them all out flush unless there are too many and crowded, because they will throw fruiting wood for the following season. All the laterals down the old limbs should be carefully thinned out if necessary, and shortened, but remember the peach bears on the new wood and much of this growth will produce good fruit this season, therefore prune for fruit. The old laterals will also have thrown out good fruiting wood and will carry some nice fruit, so prune these as required. A large proportion of the new growth will blossom and carry good fruit and with the large root system in proportion to the top, the

Fig. 149.
Heading off old Peaches for renovating.

Fig. 150.
An old unprofitable Peach.

tree will carry all the fruit it is possible to obtain without crowding it too closely for the laterals to nourish ; therefore retain all the new wood on the old limbs possible, provided it is not too crowded, in which case shorten some back to give fresh growth for the following season.

The leaders should be pruned fairly long, from eighteen inches to two feet being left, according to the growth the tree has made. Figure 153 illustrates this tree correctly pruned, while Figure 153A illustrates a tree 12 months after heading back in blossom. A glance at this tree will show how profuse the fruiting wood is and how little time is lost before a heavy crop is again obtained. Figure 154 shows a tree two years after heading back pruned and in full bearing again. This tree will be productive for many years to come and will well repay the loss of one year caused by cutting back. When renovating trees they should always be heavily

Fig. 151.
Old Peach headed back.

manured with highly nitrogenous manure and green crops should be turned under, for if the tree is not stimulated the growth will be weak.

Trees which have been split in half can often be made good by heading back and by twisting stout fencing wire round the trunks, drawing the split close together ; but first wrap a piece of sacking round the trunk to prevent the wire when tight from damaging the bark. . The main limbs should also be held firmly in place by placing a loop of strong wire round the limb on either side of the tree, using sacking as before, and twitching the wire tight with the aid of a stick. This prevents the winds from moving the join below which, if the bark is not too damaged, will heal up and grow together again. The wires should be watched and removed should the tree fill out, and new ones placed on, otherwise the tree will be strangled.

Trees which have been split can also be secured by placing a strong bolt through the trunk.

Fig. 152
Peach twelve months after heading.

Fig. 153.
The same tree pruned.

Fig. 153a.
Tree twelve months after heading back.

Fig. 154.
Peach two years after heading back.

If one side of the tree is completely broken off the other half should be headed hard back and the tree encouraged to grow over on the side lost so as to balance up the tree again as illustrated in Figure 155.

Apricots.—Apricots can be treated in the same manner as for peaches if run out, badly gummed, or broken down.

Figure 156 shows a badly gummed 12-year old apricot which was headed the previous winter. Figure 157 illustrates how this tree should be pruned.

Trees which have been neglected, as in Figure 158, should be pruned as illustrated in Figure 159. It is impossible to shape these trees properly, but the long weak leaders have been brought back, dead and cross limbs removed and the tree thinned out to allow free entry of light and air.

Fig. 155.
Renovating a tree split in half.

Practically all broken or worn out trees can be renovated in this manner if proper attention is given to manuring and cultivation afterwards. Figure 160 shows a Bartlett's Pear cut hard back ; owing to long pruning, and fruit bearing on the weak leaders this tree had become a wreck, all the leaders having broken down. Figure 161 shows the tree twelve months afterwards. The new growth has been thinned out and stout new leaders obtained on the remains of the old ones.

Unprofitable trees of poor varieties can be reworked to better sorts by heading back and either grafting on the old limbs or else budding on the new wood thrown out, but the trees must be cut hard back into the main arms for this purpose otherwise the new variety will start too high. If grafted, use the strap graft for these old limbs because it is not only a stronger and better graft but the old limb heals over quicker. Figure 162 shows how to prepare the scions. Figure163 shows the scions inserted in the old arm, the short strip being inserted under the bark on one side, the long strip is carried across the top of the old arms and inserted under the bark on the opposite side ; the long strips have just sufficient wood left in them to give strength to the bark. Figure 164 shows how the graft is tied, the strip across the top must be kept close down on the top of the old arm. Figure 165 shows all the scions in place, tied and ready for claying. Note how hard back the old tree has been cut back. Figure 166 shows the grafts properly clayed. When the grafts start all the shoots from the old butt must be removed; the shoots from the scions should be summer pruned and the young growth shaped about December or January. This strengthens them and the young growth is quickly shaped into a nice tree. Figure 167 illustrates the tree 12 months after grafting. Note how well and quickly the old sawcuts heal over, not only does the old bark callus over but the strip across the top grows to meet it. This method of grafting is a great improvement over the cleft graft and has been practised in Victoria for some years. Apples and pears can be safely grafted but it is decidedly better to bud other varieties of trees on to the new growth thrown out by the old limbs, choosing well placed and strong shoots for budding, and removing all not required.

Fig. 157.
The same tree pruned.

Fig. 156.
Apricot twelve months after heading.

130

Fig. 159.
The same tree pruned.

Fig. 158.
A neglected Apricot.

Fig. 161.
The same tree twelve months later.

Fig. 160.
Pear headed back.

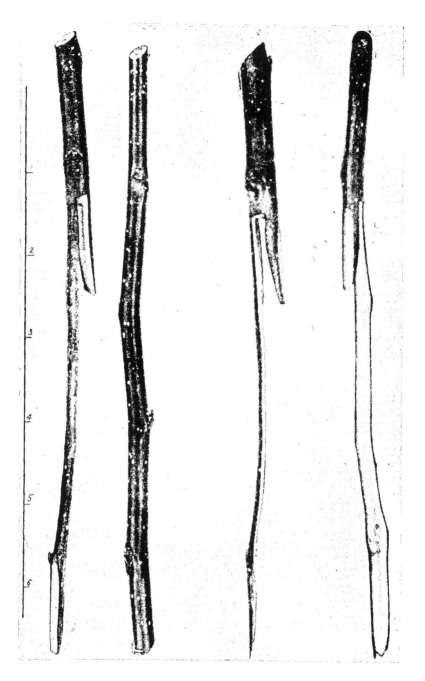

Fig. 162.
Showing how to prepare the scions.

133

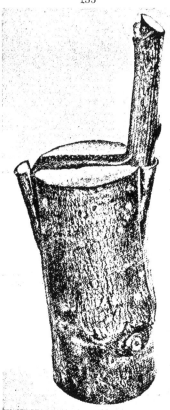

Fig. 163.
Scions inserted
in old arm.

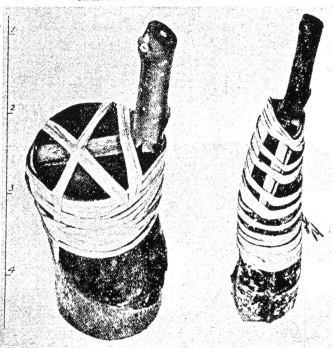

Fig. 164.

134

Fig. 165.
All scions in place and tied.

Fig. 166.

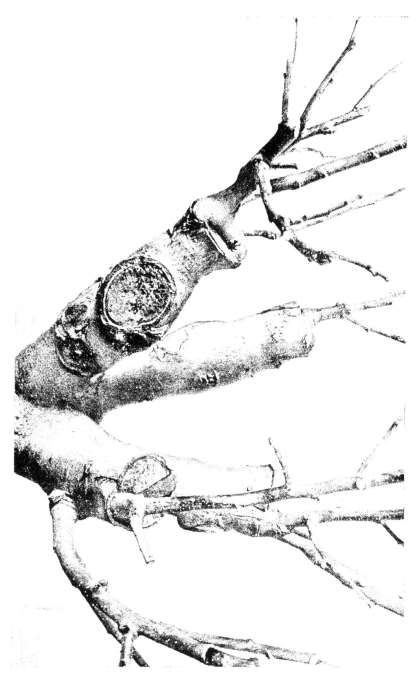

Fig. 167.
The tree twelve months after grafting.

By Authority: Fred. Wm. Simpson, Government Printer, Perth.

Printed in Great Britain
by Amazon